BEHAVIORAL SOBRIETY COACHING

Helping Others Through Recovery

Indaba Global Coaching, LLC
5050 1st Ave N.
Saint Petersburg, FL 33710
727-327-8777

www.DISCflexRecovery.com
www.BehavioralSobriety.com
www.IndabaGlobal.com

Written by Hellen Davis

Contributors: Brian Butler
Alex Fryer
James Fryer
Mike Ortega
Steven Szopinski

Editors: James Fryer

ISBN: 978-1-58570-711-2
eBook ISBN: 978-1-58570-712-0

Printed in the United States of America.

Table of Contents

I believe that wherever mastery is achieved, there's been coaching. It doesn't matter the subject; I believe people will never achieve faster success than if someone helps them, guides them, motivates them, and believes in them as they climb their mountain.

Introduction to Behavioral Sobriety™ Coaching

Behavioral Sobriety™ is the Goal.

A Certified Behavioral Sobriety™ Recovery Coach is trained to help the client realize when changes in behavior need to happen. The Behavioral Sobriety™ Recovery Program helps the client recognize that if they don't wrap their head around the new behaviors and boundaries they need and make the changes required to strive toward Behavioral Sobriety™, their future will be much like the past. Often, the coach can make inroads where trusted family members and friends cannot.

WHAT IS BEHAVIORAL SOBRIETY™?

Most experts agree that the best advice to give folks in the earliest days of recovery is: 'Don't think and don't drink'. This means that you would focus on your BEHAVIOR over your FEELINGS and EMOTIONS. This doesn't mean forever, but it does mean that your behavior should be top of mind in your recovery efforts.

The foundation of Behavioral Sobriety™ is your actions, not your feelings and emotions. Here's a good parallel: You can be livid, fuming, furious and ready to tear someone's head off their shoulders, but if you don't ACT on your emotions; and you remain calm and self-controlled, your behavior is appropriate. This is Behavioral Sobriety™. You can crave drugs, want a drink in the worst way; but if you restrain yourself, by whatever means, you are exhibiting Behavioral Sobriety™.

Behavioral Sobriety™ is based on the actions you take and the habits you form; guiding their thoughts, decision making and behaviors. If you are 'behaviorally sober', you consistently exhibit self-control or 'sober restraint'. People might perceive your overall nature as calm, being in control, doing things in moderation, abiding by appropriate boundaries, restricting unwise behaviors, having command of your actions and/or having a sense of self-discipline. When you exhibit Behavioral Sobriety™ you do not allow yourself to be overcome with emotion, especially negative ones.

If you lack Behavioral Sobriety™, you might over-react – leaping to judgment, making decisions that run against recovery efforts, or those that harm relationships. In terms of the Love-Hurt-Anger Cycle, you might overreact; going from deeply caring, to hurt, to highly upset, at warp speed. It takes you a nanosecond to roar. When this happens, you are typically unable to self-regulate. You've already launched! Most disturbing, you lose your ability to fine-tune your actions. In terms of DISCflex Factors, you've lost the ability to 'dial up' or 'dial down' your behavioral components; getting them (through self-regulation) to a place where they are behaviorally appropriate for the situation.

The first step of Behavioral Sobriety™ is physical sobriety – giving up addictive substances. The second step is behaving in a way that shows the traits of sobriety.

WHAT IS A BEHAVIORAL SOBRIETY™ COACH?

Addictions often become so ingrained that a person's brain automatically turns to negative self-defeating behaviors and habits. As a Behavioral Sobriety™ Coach, you'll help your clients understand their underlying natural behavior and how these can help lift them or potentially hurt their recovery efforts. Looking at the definition of Behavioral Sobriety™, most people simply don't know where to turn to get this type of education or help for themselves or those they love. This is a fundamental reason for why people need the assistance of a Behavioral Sobriety™ Coach with a structured and logic program, especially in the first stages of their recovery efforts. Additionally, if you chose to encompass a holistic supporter and family-based approach, you can provide insight into the family dynamics, too. Often, recovery efforts can be significantly enhanced by providing insight into the contributing 'relationship factor dynamics' in the client's life.

> To have long-term success as a coach or in any position of leadership, you have to be obsessed in some way.
>
> -Pat Riley

COACHING METHODOLOGY

Certified Behavioral Sobriety™ Coaches provide a sounding board for their clients as they engage in their recovery journey. Most important, they provide models of excellence, a proven process, and knowledge for their coaches to follow so that they work toward Behavioral Sobriety™.

Unlike other coaching methodologies, we do not believe the client has all the answers. We believe that no one has all the answers for the things they face in recovery. With that guiding principle, we not only ask probing questions, we help the client walk through options, and ask them to explore the consequences of decision making. Most importantly, we look at their behavior as a driver for attaining Behavioral Sobriety™ to provide suggestions, options, and education to help in this realm.

A BEHAVIORAL SOBRIETY™ COACH PROVIDES EDUCATION SO THAT CLIENTS CAN ADJUST OR 'TUNE INTO' THEIR HABITS.

Flexing behavior to the situations people face is an extremely important skillset: Behavior is what causes action. Repeated ingrained actions are habits. Think of the way to tune into all of your habits as if you are a radio. Each station is a different habit. By raising or lowering the frequency dial (dialing up and dialing down), you can 'set' your station (your behavior) for whatever situation you are facing. This way of thinking sets the tone for acquiring Behavioral Sobriety™. We have proven for more than three decades that behavioral change is possible in any arena of life – from communicating effectively, dealing with anger, handling grief, working with different people, and just about any life skill imaginable. With the appropriate knowledge and guidance, clients can acquire this proficiency.

The coach helps the clients walk through their recovery goals in appropriate timelines. A Recovery Coach also stresses the need for introspection and self-examination, resulting in a rational and critical approach to solving ethical dilemmas and problems. They help the client clarify their thinking by asking probing questions, listening intently for both intent and decision making that will result in actions, behaviors and habits. The coach is trained to provide clear definitions of basic concepts. They provide insight into the client's natural behavior patterns and explain the behaviors vital for recovery. Most important, they track progress and provide a standard for accountability.

HISTORY

Our DISCflex™ Recovery founders started our coaching organization more than 30 years ago. Philosophically we are quite different from other coaching associations and organizations. Our foundational belief is that Certified Behavioral Sobriety™ Coaches best serve their clients when they can fully engage; when they bring a wealth of experience to their coaching engagements. The specific goal for the client is to attain a working knowledge of what it takes to achieve Behavioral Sobriety™.

BEHAVIORAL SOBRIETY™ COACHING PHILOSOPHY & MISSION

Philosophically as Behavioral Sobriety™ Coaches, we are quite different from other coaching associations and organizations. Our foundational belief is that a Behavioral Sobriety™ Coach best serves their clients when they can fully engage; when they bring a wealth of experience to their coaching engagements. A Behavioral Sobriety™ Coach's mission is to encourage clients to think about their behavior and habits; while always stressing the need for analytical self-examination, for clear definitions of basic concepts, and for a rational and critical approach to solving ethical dilemmas, approaching opportunities, and solving problems.

Behavioral Sobriety™ Coaches provide a sounding board for their clients as they engage in philosophical dialogue tuned to recovery efforts. Most important, they provide models of excellence and knowledge for their clients to follow so that they complete goals faster and continue with their recovery efforts. When a Behavioral Sobriety™ Coach brings their passion and wealth of their experience to the table, they often find that they perform services that are not purely in the traditional coaching realm by supplying insight, support, guidance, information, relaying material on resource providers, and recommending educational materials.

ROLES OF A BEHAVIORAL SOBRIETY™ COACH

You can take on various roles in your client's recovery efforts. If your client is afraid of failing in their struggle with addiction, a Behavioral Sobriety™ Coach can guide them toward a clearer path forward, perhaps even helping with those first critical steps. When a client is ready to confront addictive behaviors and work to change their habits, you can show them alternatives that might work. You can provide insight and experience to build their hope that success is possible for them. Here are some of the roles a Behavioral Sobriety™ Coach may take on:

- Listener
- Question Asker
- Educator
- Feedback Giver
- Supporter
- Advocate
- Motivator
- Accountability Person
- Alternative Suggester
- Structure Contributor
- Courage Coach (when they need to overcome their fears)

BEHAVIORAL SOBRIETY™ USING A STRUCTURED AND LOGICAL APPROACH

As a Behavioral Sobriety™ Coach, you'll take your clients through a structured program to help your client work to develop new and healthy behaviors. New thinking, new behavior and new habits need

structure to 'gel and stick'. By working through their 'Book About Me' workbook (and with you providing insight and feedback), your client will put together specific actions that support their recovery efforts and life's goals. They discuss decision making and how their natural behavior patterns impact their actions and habits. With your guidance and feedback, they'll come up with alternatives to addiction. Having a quick solution ready when they crave their old habits builds their strength to change.

MEASURING SUCCESS FOR COACHING SESSIONS

Success isn't measured by:

- The client's positive feelings toward, and relationship with, the Behavioral Sobriety™ Coach. **True success is measured by results of changes in behavior and ongoing adherence to behavioral parameters and goal accomplishment.**

- How well the client performs with the Recovery Coach's direct assistance or help. **Success is measured by how well the client performs when the Recovery Coach is not present.**
- How clients 'feel' about their own progress. **Success must be measured by changes others perceive in the client's behavior.**

WHY USE THE BEHAVIORAL SOBRIETY™ RECOVERY PROGRAM?

We understand that Recovery Coaches are engaged by clients for a variety of reasons and that there is no one-size-fits-all Recovery Coaching model. However, in producing this program, we discovered there is a universal 'common thread' that is found in successful recovery efforts. In particular, we have found that behavior and habits that focus on reducing cognitive dissonance, defining appropriate boundaries, goal setting, decision making, Self-Talk, and accountability are the foundations of most successful recovery efforts. The Behavioral Sobriety™ Program helps the coach lead the client through a logical, thoughtful and planned approach to behavior-based recovery efforts. Our team spent years developing this behavior- and habit-based approach with the assistance and feedback from some of the best minds in the recovery community.

WHAT MAKES THE BEHAVIORAL SOBRIETY™ COACHING PROGRAM DIFFERENT?

A Certified Behavioral Sobriety™ Coach's tasks are to encourage clients to think for themselves and provide models of excellence throughout the Behavioral Sobriety™ Recovery Program. By introducing new information, we know that the client will experience significant amounts of cognitive dissonance. The activities in the 'Book

About Me' workbook will help the client process through this. The workbook outlines a foundational program to underpin the coaching assignment by providing structure and accountability for the client.

USING THE HOPE/PAIN MATRIX TO ENHANCE RECOVERY EFFORTS

We have been training coaches for decades. We realize that while all coaching shares some common principles, Behavioral Sobriety™ Coaching focuses on two key areas that might not be as critical in management, leadership or life coaching:

H.O.P.E

hold on, pain ends.

1. Increasing hope for the future to drive motivation.
2. Decreasing the pain associated with past addiction by using targeted reflection and discovery to drive healing and forgiveness.

By using the Hope-Pain Accountability Matrix we can plot a client's progress as they work through their recovery efforts. We believe that a client's ability to function in the situations they encounter, as well as the behaviors they exhibit as they face these, affect hope and pain. Lack of appropriate functioning skills causes pain. Inappropriate behavior makes clients think don't/can't 'fit in'. Building appropriate behavioral skills that lead to better habits increases hope.

By focusing on the Hope/Pain Matrix, and by using cognitive dissonance principles, we provide a logical and systematic approach that provides the client with education and tools vital to their recovery efforts. The goal is to reduce any cognitive dissonance that occurs as a natural result of the client going through the Behavioral Sobriety™ Coaching Process. Together with their Behavioral Sobriety™ Coach the client will explore the steps necessary for their goals. When a Behavioral Sobriety™ Coach brings the wealth of their experience to the table, they often perform services that are not purely in the traditional coaching realm. They provide insight, suggestions, resources, and valuable information to their clients.

HOW DOES BEHAVIORAL SOBRIETY™ COACHING WORK?

Increasing hope and decreasing pain require a 'shift in thinking'. Often, people are never taught precisely how to make a 'mental shift' as well as an 'actions shift'. Often the reason that recovery efforts don't 'stick' is that these two don't line up. Even if the person wants to quit destructive behaviors and truly desires a better life, they just don't have the knowledge, tools, or accountability coach to get there. That's why becoming a Behavioral Sobriety™ Coach is so important. As a Behavioral Sobriety™ Coach, you'll have the tools, skills, assessments and program to hold the client accountable for taking on the education necessary to their journey.

> Coaching is unlocking a person's potential to maximize their own goals and capabilities. It's helping them learn, rather than teaching them.

As a Behavioral Sobriety™ Coach, you can help your clients 'hold up their mirror' in a productive way that people too close to the client and/or the situation often can't. You'll help your clients understand that a monumental 'shift in thinking' followed by short- and long-term shifts in behavior can indeed create healthier habits. You can help motivate them and hold them accountable because this 'shift' takes time and concentrated effort. When the client becomes discouraged, experiences internal anguish or loses hope again, you, as their coach, can be their sounding board, supporter, as well as their 'accountability person'. Many times, shifting these vital elements from family members to you preserves family and friendship bonds.

One of the most important goals you have as a Recovery Coach's is to the monitor the levels of cognitive dissonance the client is experiencing. The Behavioral Sobriety™ Program will teach you precisely how this works. As a Recovery Coach, you will coach/ guide/motivate the client towards reconciliation of the dissonance they are experiencing. Specifically, you'll take the client through the self-discovery process to 'square with' who the client was/is versus the future the client envisions.

BRINGING YOUR EXPERIENCE AND 'SPECIAL SAUCE' TO THE TABLE

We know that the most successful coaches in the world combine their worldly experiences with a proven process that drives client accountability. As a Behavioral Sobriety™ Coach, you can use the guidelines and program to bring what you have learned through formal (classroom and conventional education) and informal training (life experiences) to the table. Keeping true to your personal values and mission as a coach is vitally important to your authenticity, mission and purpose. All the knowledge and education provided in the program, including the activities, can (and should) be blended with your 'special sauce'. Your 'special sauce' is what draws clients to you. Your unique style, personal values, purpose, and experience should always be at the core of your practice. The Behavioral Sobriety™ Recovery Program allows for you to 'be you' while providing a foundation and proven process for coaching success.

Coaching

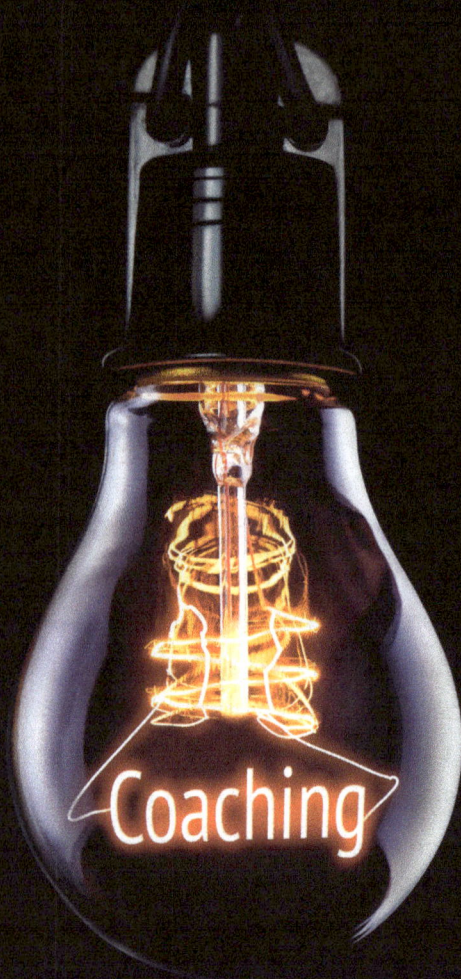

I am a coach because I believe in people's ability to overcome anything, to rise above their current circumstances and achieve whatever their heart and head desire. There's no better feeling than seeing someone I coach 'get it'. I love seeing their light bulb go on! If they understand the importance of discipline, build their success through education and hard work, are determined to carry on because I helped stimulate their 'motivation muscle'; that's the reward that no one but a coach will ever truly understand. It fuels my being!

The Basis for Coaching

In your first coaching session, you should have already completed your personal DISC assessment, so you know who you are. This way you know what behaviors you'll have to flex as you look at each of your clients' DISC scores. It's important to be able to 'flex' to build trust and communicate effectively in every coaching session.

Topic of Discussion Triangle

In each coaching session, we recommend that you explain this concept and its importance.

The basis for the coaching process looks like a triangle.

SOLUTION, NEXT STEPS, AND ACCOUNTABILITY

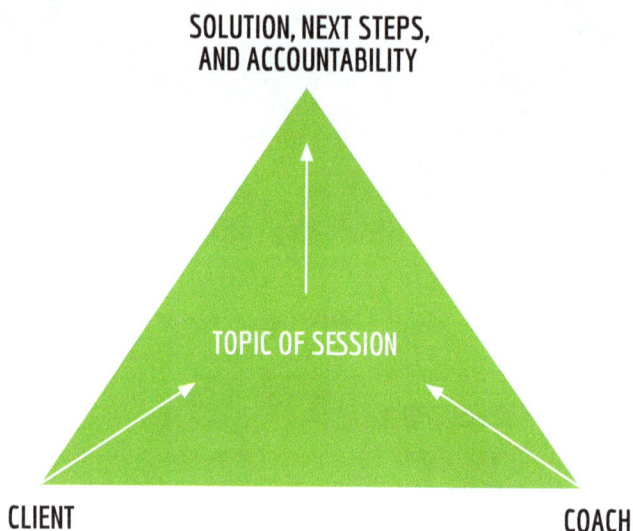

TOPIC OF SESSION

CLIENT   COACH

THE BASE

At the base of the triangle, are two people: 1. the client on one side and 2. the recovery coach on the other. There is a distinctive separation between the two people. This is important so that the issues like transference, conflicts of interest, imposing value systems on each other, etc. do not occur.

THE CENTER OF THE TRIANGLE

Additionally, clients might not want to talk about the topic (problem, opportunity, challenge or issue) of the session for a variety of reasons. However, where the coach focuses the session's attention has significant impact on recovery efforts. Ensuring that the topic of the session stays at the forefront will keep the client and coach focused on what they need to cover for that session. If a topic enters the session's discussion that is not appropriate for the topic of session or is scheduled to be discussed later up in the program, it can be handled in a variety of ways:

1. The issue can be put in a parking lot for the end of the session.
2. It can be scheduled for later date.
3. Additional coaching time can be allocated.

THE APEX

At the apex of the triangle is mutually agreed to be the best approach and the accountability parameters around that solution. You and the client will discuss specific behaviors and actions that need to be accomplished for the client to move forward with their recovery efforts. The key to an effective coaching session, are to document the actions and desired behaviors with appropriate timelines.

The substance of the triangle is the discussion topic for the session.

- This substance could be a topic that contains a problem, opportunity, challenge or issue.
- It could be that the client needs to have education around the model or topic area.

Running Your Coaching Sessions

As a Behavioral Sobriety™ Coach, how you run and prepare for your coaching sessions is critical to yours and your client's success.

PREPARATION

1. Get all the information you can about your client prior to all your sessions and keep updating this information. How? Review their recent activity on web sites, blogs, Twitter, Facebook, and LinkedIn. Check in with friends and family and remember the coaching guidelines for confidentiality and protocol.

2. State the purpose of the coaching sessions at the beginning of each session. Ask the client if they have anything to add to the coaching session agenda. Clients may interrupt, distract, or sabotage coaching sessions if they're not given an opportunity to share their concerns. Get these concerns out at the start, so that the focus can then go to the coaching session's purpose. You might ask: What has transpired since we last met that you'd like to share? What goals or feelings keep bubbling up when you think about the purpose of this coaching session?

3. State the outcome you seek for the coaching session. If you don't have a clear purpose and outcome, what's to keep your coaching sessions from going off the rails?

4. Select a venue or communication means that meets yours and your client's needs. Make sure that you stock it with the

basics (see Checklist for Coaching Sessions Meeting Room below). Prior to every coaching session check on the room's condition prior to meeting with the client. Some Recovery Coaches go so far as to check for beverage preferences and to see if the room has any flickering lights beforehand. At the very least, you want to make sure that the room can accommodate your technology needs. You might also want to make sure there's sugar on hand, since glucose enhances concentration.

5.   Walk through the coaching session's agenda, any meeting rules, and send out any reading material in advance that might 'tee up' the coaching session. The agenda should allocate time for each agenda item, based upon importance. Ground rules and agendas provide structure and expectations of conduct. Since coaching sessions are designed for conversation, make it clear what clients are expected to read, bring with them, and/or review before the coaching session.

6.   Always build or reestablish trust and rapport prior to launching 'the meat' of the coaching session. Craft warm-up questions that will draw out any hidden agendas or 'check ups'.

7.   Prepare a list of open-ended questions to draw out opinions and ideas. Sometimes quiet clients need a little coaxing. You might ask: What alternative approaches have we looked at that you're not fully on board with yet? What would your xxx's response be? What if it doesn't work? Who else should we talk to before moving forward?

8.   Anticipate post-meeting reluctances to follow through with commitments made, and head them off. Clients often say what they want you to hear but when the coaching sessions is over; their actions tell what they really think. 'Reluctance conversations' can diminish or undermine the client's recovery efforts. Ask a cool-down question at the end of the coaching sessions to capture the essence of client's feelings and concerns about commitments they've made during the session. You might ask: As you think through what you've promised to do, what's something you wanted to address but did not see an opportunity to bring it up? What do you think will be most challenging going forward? When you go home tonight, what will you share about our coaching sessions, if anything, with your spouse or friends?

GROUND RULES FOR COACHING SESSIONS

Here are basic principles that should be clarified for all coaching sessions:

- Start and end on time.
- Focus on behaviors, without judgement, and facilitate honest sharing about progress.
- Respect each other's ideas, thoughts and opinions.
- Respect confidentiality (What is discussed in the sessions, stays in the coaching sessions unless mutually agreed to share).
- Agree to participate fully during the coaching session and to be 'present'.
- Confidentiality, expectation, ethics considerations, and commitment will remain consistent throughout all coaching sessions.
- Discuss any changes to progress reporting relationships and communication parameters.
- Methods of information gathering are transparent.
- Attempt to make wise judgements, participate in prudent decision making, set objectives and monitor progress toward recovery efforts.

CHECKLIST FOR YOUR COACHING SESSION MEETING ROOM

- Box for 'checking' phones.
- Water or other appropriate beverages
- Your choice of snacks/food
- Tissues
- Paper
- Pens and pencils
- Computer (to allow the client to take assessments and for delivering lessons/PowerPoints)
- Means for projecting educational materials
- Post the coaching sessions Ground Rules.
- Temperature should be monitored.
- Lighting should be appropriate.
- Sounds and other disturbances should be kept to a minimum.
- Ideally the venue should be private and away from 'other ears'.

Advocacy

As a Behavioral Sobriety Coach, it is your responsibility to advocate for the client while teaching them how to advocate for themselves. This may include giving suggestions based on boundaries including: family, work, friends, and other relationships in their lives. It is not your responsibility to set boundaries for them, but again, to assist them in learning how to do so. This may include teaching the client how to be assertive in high-risk situations in their lives that may lead to relapse. If your client is involved in legal matters, they may ask you to attend their court hearing with them and this is highly encouraged as it shows support. Also, in advocating, they may need assistance with resources in their local area. This may require you to speak on their behalf but before doing so, make sure you have read the and abide by all privacy and confidentiality laws, rules and regulations and apply to your coaching practice. As an example, in the USA, be certain to abide by HIPPA laws pertaining to your jurisdiction.

HIPPA/Confidentiality – HIPPA is a law designed to protect the client information from anyone other than the company the client is dealing with. There are some exceptions when breaking client confidentiality and confidential information. It is strongly suggested that you become familiar with your government's regulations and laws regarding HIPPA as there are several variations. For more information please research your state or nation's government regulations regarding client/patient confidentiality.

Cultures

Behavioral Sobriety Coaching serves all cultures, subcultures, and even countercultures. A culture is a set of morals, values, traditions, and practices shared by society or group for the greater good of a community and society. A subculture is a branch of a culture with a group of people who have developed their own beliefs and values while still adhering to the norms, guiding principles, and/or laws of the greater culture. A counterculture is a group of individuals within a culture whose views oppose the beliefs and values of the larger culture. A counter culture is defiant of the social norms that are accepted in the larger society.

The understanding of the 3 types of cultures is important for a Behavioral Sobriety Coach because different families come from different environments containing different beliefs and practices. It is important during the first session of coaching to get to know the client and find out what type of beliefs and traditions he/she had growing up. Having this information can heighten the coach's awareness to be more in tune with the individual's behavior and experiences. The goal for culture discussions is to get greater insight into the client's background. Having this insight also helps remind the coach to be respectful of the individual's upbringing. Remember: Building trust with your client builds the foundation for them to confide in you so that you may assist them in their recovery process.

Bottom line: You are not to judge a person's culture, background, education, status, values or practices even if you don't agree with them.

I'm the person who tells you what you don't want to hear, shows you what you don't want to see, won't listen to your excuses, so you can be who you've always known you can be. I can help you unlock your potential.

- Hellen Davis

UNLOCK YOU
POTENTIAL

Cognitive Dissonance

What causes people to behave the way they do as they strive for new recovery-based behaviors?

Natural behavior patterns are set early in life. A Behavioral Sobriety™ Coach will walk their client through the 'Report About Me' which will create awareness of the underlying natural behaviors the client has. These underlying natural behavior patterns are a combination of nature (traits you were born with) and nurture (caused by what factors played a part in your upbringing). Having these natural behaviors doesn't mean that they don't play a big part in how people address recovery efforts. Most important in creating new recovery-based behaviors and habits, is the roles that stress, decision making and consequence awareness play.

Critical to creating new behaviors and habits is awareness of the concept of **cognitive dissonance**. Cognitive dissonance is the mental discomfort (psychological stress) people feel when they have choices to make, things to work through, or when they are juggling two competing thoughts that don't 'get along together'. These fight with each other and cause internal stress. Often, cognitive dissonance happens a person does/has done something that goes directly against what they know is the right thing to do according to their core values, beliefs, and ideals. This is central to what happens when people are impacted by addiction. The person must come to terms with the consequences of their behaviors and a large component of the stress they'll deal with is reconciling their past actions with who they were, their current view of who they are, and painting their new future landscape.

To complicate matters in the recovery process, cognitive dissonance also happens when new information is added that will impact the way a person has to begin to think or behave in their future. To function and succeed in any recovery program, people must resolve cognitive dissonance from their past and work on it to move forward to a brighter tomorrow.

COMING TO TERMS WITH THE PAST AND BUILDING A NEW FUTURE

To 'win' the internal battle and 'fix' what's causing stress, people must 'patch up' their relationship with themselves. This is difficult for someone to do when they're in the habit of beating themselves up. **People must find a way to square with what they've done and where they can go in life as they move forward with their recovery efforts.** To do this, they must have dependability and consistency between their personal expectations of life and their actions. **This means they must be guided through the process of systematically reducing cognitive dissonance.** That's where a Behavioral Sobriety™ Coach comes in. A Behavioral Sobriety™ Coach will help set up the educational components necessary to understand this concept and will build on it by supplying models to build their client's life skills.

Being a 'cheerleader coach' isn't enough.

A Behavioral Sobriety™ Coach knows it takes a proven process to stay in recovery. The Behavioral Sobriety™ Coach will explain the importance of practicing the process of 'dissonance reduction' to make sure their client understands how they can continually align cognitions (perceptions of the world) with their actions, attitudes, and habits. To accomplish this, they'll take their client through a rigorous process of self-discovery, education, and accountability, while motivating them in their recovery efforts.

MOST PEOPLE AREN'T ABLE TO LIFT THEMSELVES OUT OF ADDICTION WITHOUT KNOWLEDGE AND HELP

Cognitive dissonance is something that most people don't even realize is happening. It's quite amazing because cognitive dissonance happens consistently whenever we are faced with something that 'seems not right', is something we are uncomfortable with, or whenever we face something we need to think through before making decisions about what to do next or acting. It's as common a mental function as breathing! But whether you understand and recognize it or not, the ramifications of staying in a 'state of cognitive dissonance' creates mental stress, anguish and often results in poor decision making if people don't recognize it's happening or have a way to work through it. This is precisely where a Behavioral Sobriety™ Coach can assist the client in understanding what is happening.

Cognitive Dissonance: The Theory

Almost half a century ago social psychologist Leon Festinger developed the Cognitive Dissonance Theory (Festinger, 1957). The theory is mentioned in most general and social psychology textbooks today, so obviously it's valuable because it stood the test of time. It addresses the persistent human tendency to rationalize and justify.

Cognitive dissonance theory is based on three fundamental assumptions:

People are sensitive to inconsistencies between actions and beliefs. When inconsistencies happen, internal bells and whistles go off like alarms. This is an automatic response. If you think it's wrong to lie, but you tell a lie to a friend, no matter how small, your mind sends out a signal telling you something's not right with what's happening.

Awareness of the inconsistency will motivate the person to resolve the issue. If you know you've violated a core principle, you must figure out a reason why and justify it to yourself. Your justification must be stronger than the uncomfortable feeling you're trying to overcome. (You try to say it was ok to do it, and then you're good with it and can move on.) The degree to which your beliefs and values conflict with your actions, is the barometer of how much dissonance (uncomfortableness) you'll feel. Also, the greater the dissonance, the more you will be motivated to resolve it.

THE DISSONANCE WILL BE RESOLVED IN ONE OF THREE BASIC WAYS:

1. **Change your core value and/or beliefs:** For example, just decide that lying is o.k. This would take care of any dissonance. However, this is by far the hardest for most people because core values and beliefs get locked it early and 'stick'.
2. **Change actions:** Decide that you'll never lie again and stick to it. This takes a lot of reminding and willpower!
3. **Change your perception of what you did:** You could reframe what you did in more acceptable terms. It was 'just a white lie' and 'didn't hurt anyone'. In this way you think about what you did differently so that it no longer appears to be; inconsistent with your actions. If you reflect on this series of mental gymnastics for a moment you will probably recognize why cognitive dissonance has come to be so popular.

Through our certification programs, you will grow in experience. Becoming certified in the Behavioral Sobriety™ Recovery Program will significantly enrich your coaching practice. What will set you apart from other coaches is your methodology and accountability practices including the fully validated DISCflex™ Recovery tools, and Behavioral Sobriety™ Recovery Program centered on the 'Report About Me' and 'Book About Me' workbook. By taking clients through their recovery journey focusing on the skills and knowledge they'll gain in the Behavioral Sobriety™ Recovery Program, you'll be able to scale your coaching practice. You'll be able to spend more time coaching and acquiring clients than on 'build out'. This means you'll achieve revenue goals that most coaches only dream about.

HOPE/PAIN MATRIX

As your client focuses on meeting their recovery goals, working on the changes they need to make in their behaviors and habits, their objective must be to continue to be a fully functioning and participating member of society. They should strive to behave in a manner they and others can be proud of. The more success they see in this area, the better they will feel about themselves. This decreases pain and increases hope. they will begin to achieve levels of success in their recovery efforts. The Hope/Pain Matrix was derived from a well-known Early Stage Recovery Model.

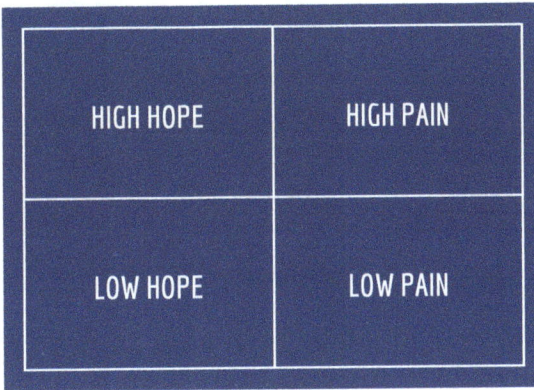

HIGH HOPE	HIGH PAIN
LOW HOPE	LOW PAIN

However, we found that coaching to the original concept was problematic. This well-recognized model, while intuitive, is not appropriate for driving accountability. The Hope and Pain axes in the original model are inherently 'process contradictory' meaning it is impossible to for a client to work towards the top right-hand box of the model. This progression is important for operating models. The goal is to work toward lowering pain and increasing hope in an orderly progression through a Behavior-based Treatment Plan focused on KSAs (knowledge, skills, attitude).

How did we modify the model?

By adjusting the axes and linking behavior to the Hope Axis and Pain to the Functioning Axis, the Behavioral Sobriety™ Coaching Program created the appropriate process for coaching sessions that drive toward lowering pain and increasing hope.

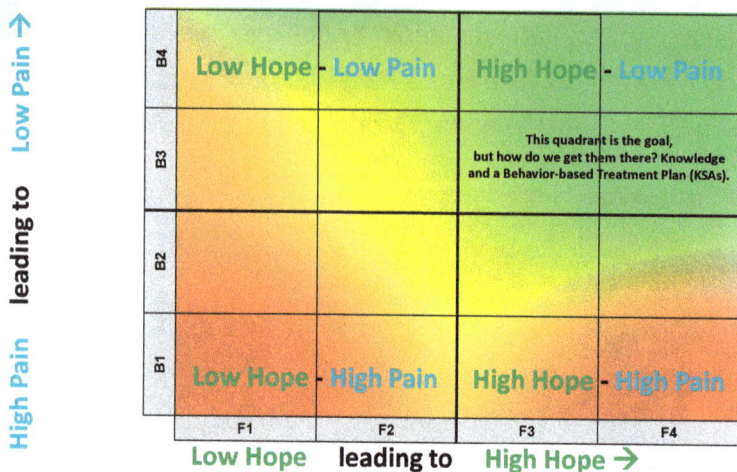

B4	Low Hope - Low Pain	High Hope - Low Pain	
B3		This quadrant is the goal, but how do we get them there? Knowledge and a Behavior-based Treatment Plan (KSAs).	
B2			
B1	Low Hope - High Pain	High Hope - High Pain	
	F1 Low Hope	F2 leading to	F3 High Hope →

Low Pain ↑ leading to High Pain (vertical axis)

INCREASED HOPE AND DECREASED PAIN AS MOTIVATORS AND DRIVERS

By using the Hope-Pain Accountability Matrix, a Recovery Coach can plot a client's progress as they work through their recovery efforts. This proven methodology shows how a client can progress systematically through their recovery efforts using Hope and Pain as motivators and drivers, building behavioral and functioning skills as they progress.

A client's ability to function in the situations they encounter, as well as the behaviors they exhibit as they face these, affect hope and pain. Lack of appropriate functioning skills causes pain. Inappropriate behavior makes clients think they don't/can't 'fit in'. This is an illusion that the many clients often operate under. This may lead to self-loathing, a lack of self-confidence, and self-pity. Building appropriate behavioral skills that lead to better habits increases hope.

The process outlines the consequences of staying in one of the Hope/Pain Matrix boxes without making progress. It demonstrates how a client without proper behavioral skills, habits, and awareness can be just as damaging to themselves and those around them as a highly mature person with little awareness of what the 'functioning expectations' of the group are at all! More important, the model underscores the necessity of working simultaneously on behavior and functioning capabilities.

Recovery coaching success is noticeable when the client strives to possess strong functioning skills, is engaged in the education process, and wants to achieve a level of behavioral intelligence whereby the client becomes a trusted and respected member of society. Please remember that a coach's success is not necessarily tied to the client's actions. An old saying comes to mind: "You can lead a horse to water, but you can't make them drink."

CLIENTS WILL ACHIEVE A HIGH LEVEL OF SUCCESS IN THEIR RECOVERY EFFORTS WHEN THEY ARE WILLING TO:

- Examine themselves and look at what actions and habits they want.
- Assess other people's reasonable expectations of them.
- Put their ego and emotions aside. (be objective) I think this word should be introduced along with putting ego and emotions aside as it will be used a lot in the coaching arena.
- Take in feedback.
- Make necessary changes.
- Help others who are struggling, and ultimately
- Teach others what they've learned and give back.

Assessing Where the Client is on the Hope/Pain Matrix

When coaching clients using the Hope/Pain Matrix, **it is important to be honest in your assessment of the** client's current Functioning and Behavior skills on separate scales. Once you have independently assessed each level, refer back to the Hope Pain **Model to see where they are, and how they can improve.**

WHY BEHAVIOR MATTERS

When a client acts in ways that are more consistent with their desired core values, their hope for some better future increases. **Appropriate behavior drives hope.**

Behavior plays a key role in recovery efforts, but it is rarely formally taught. Often people in the early stages of recovery have behavioral issues when it comes to situational awareness, flexibility and self-awareness - as any supporter or Recovery Coach knows! In fact, if asked what keeps them up at night; coaches will tell you it's issues around client behavior! Looking at the Behavior Indexing chart, you can easily assess where you think the client is with their recovery efforts because there are clear delineations between the levels. The 'Book About Me' workbook will help lead the client through behavioral models and education they probably haven't concentrated enough on.

BEHAVIOR INDEXING™

Level	Four Levels to Satisfy Your Recovery Efforts
B4	**Have Passion and Encourage Others** (Service) – Be a Role Model – Willing and able to support friends, family, peers, counselors, and supporters. Walk the walk; talk the talk.
B3	**Set Ego Aside** (Releasing Control) - Take Others into Consideration – Use this critical knowledge to adjust your behavior if necessary. Make conscious effort to fit your behavior to every situation; and/or work on habits ('morphing' over the long term). Work diligently to interact and communicate more effectively, with greater confidence, yielding better overall results.
B2	**Understand Your Impact on Others** (3rd Party Perception) – EXACTLY how your peers view you. Adapting your behavior is the key to success. People may see you one way, while you might have an entirely different view. This difference in perception is the root cause of conflict, misunderstandings, mistrust, and ultimately can cause an abundance of problems.
B1	**Understand How Self-Perception Affects Us** (Self-Awareness) – We judge ourselves (good and bad). Take measure of yourself objectively. **The first step is to complete your DISCflex assessment.** Willing to take a measure of who you are based on things you value and your expectations of how you should behave as you start your recovery efforts. This process culminates in self-perception. Self-judgment and judgment of others cannot be easily stopped; and our actions, communication, and attitude are determined and influenced by it.

WHY BEING ABLE TO FUNCTION MATTERS:

When a client is able to function according to expectations (theirs and others) their pain decreases. Frustration decreases, pride and self-confidence increase. **Functioning well drives meaningfulness, purpose and defines their role as a member of society.** Looking at the Functioning Indexing chart, you can easily assess where you think the client is with their recovery efforts because there are clear delineations between the levels. The activities in the 'Book About Me' workbook help build the client's functioning capacity by teaching them core principles.

FUNCTIONING INDEX™

Level	Four Levels to Satisfy Your Recovery Program
F4	**Teach Someone Else and Support Their Recovery Efforts** – Being able to teach someone what you've learned is important.
F3	**Implement Plan and Measure Progress (Accountability)** – Setting proper accountability guidelines and analyzing results is essential to building your competencies.
F2	**Set Goals** – You must set recovery goals before you can gain an understanding of where functional gaps lie.
F1	**Uncover Expectations** – Be willing to start recovery efforts. The first thing is to identify responsibilities and expectations, complete your SWOT analysis. This will increase awareness of how your recovery efforts will benefit you and those you care about.

NAVIGATING BEHAVIOR

Behavior is often difficult to talk about because most people don't understand how behaviors work and habits 'stick'. DISCflex Recovery Assessments and the 'Report About Me' help clients move through the Hope/Pain Matrix because it is a roadmap for recovery efforts. When you explain the Hope/Pain Matrix to clients, they'll understand it is a distinct process to assessing behavior and their skills and functioning abilities in a methodical way.

When you look at the Hope/Pain Matrix charts in this section, you'll see why this Hope/Pain Matrix Process is so important! If a client looks like they are at the B1 and B2 level, you can ascertain whether they are able to start to focus on setting their ego aside and take others into consideration (B3). The 'Report About Me' and the 'Book About Me' workbook help teach the client about their behavior, pattern, style, strengths, weaknesses, decision making, and ways of looking at their situation. It details how their communication might affect others' opinions about them (B1). Clients will also be able to invite others to take a 3rd Party Assessment about their behaviors to find out how others perceive them (B2). Using the self-perception hand-in-hand with the 3rd party assessment results, a client can get a better understanding of where they are today vs where they want to be tomorrow.

Hope/Pain Matrix Case Study

OVERVIEW

Recovery Coaches often look for the quickest and most effective way to point a client in the 'right' direction for their recovery efforts. With the limited amount of time, budget, and resources available, ramping the skills and capabilities of someone new in their recovery efforts is often a difficult task. Both the client and Recovery Coach recognize the importance of pulling up behavior and functioning skills, and they are open to finding a solution most suitable to incorporating both of those concepts into their coaching sessions.

Looking at the Hope/Pain Matrix, the Recovery Coach knows they have to motivate their client to two different points in the matrix

H.O.P.E.

HOLD ON, PAIN ENDS

(boxes) during their recovery efforts. As the coaching sessions progress, the Recovery Coach has to figure out how to leverage both the functioning skills and behaviors of their client at appropriate points in their development. In particular, the Recovery Coach needs to track the client's development.

The Recovery Coach has to be systematic in their approach as they motivate their client toward the next level of growth. By using the Hope/Pain Matrix as their guideline, the Recovery Coach can make an assessment, formulate a coaching plan, and track their client's progress. The goal is to have a series of orderly behavior and skills development moments that progress the client through the Hope/Pain Matrix. By incorporating the appropriate aspects of functioning/skills and behavior, the Recovery Coach can track client's progress as they move farther up and to the right on the Hope/Pain Matrix.

PROBLEM

In Behavioral Sobriety™ Coaching, the Recovery Coach consistently encounters four overarching difficulties while running their practice. It is best to try to overcome these so that you can run effective coaching sessions:

- A lack of knowledge or training in behavior and skills.
- Pricing and marketing skills and the time management skills to accomplish these.
- Know-how in fleshing out client expectations incorporating a format for continued follow-up including checking accountability metrics.
- Onboarding/starting new clients with various start dates and different coaching needs.

Also, a Recovery Coach needs to plot where they want their clients to be on the chart based on the client's willingness, skills, current behavior and experience. Then, the Recovery Coach needs to plot where their clients need to be in the appropriate time periods. The Recovery Coach has to decide:

- Should they work on adjusting client's behaviors first and then ramp up the functioning aspect? Or vice versa?
- Is it actually possible to do both at the same time? Would the time be best spent working on both simultaneously?
- What are the pros/cons of each approach?
- Would you use the same coach/mentor, or can you ask for assistance from a supporter or require attendance at recovery meetings to supplement recovery efforts?

- What are your options?
- What are the appropriate timelines? How can we best track skills progress and behavioral progress (or lack thereof) against timeline expectations?

SOLVE

1. Based on your experience, what should the Recovery Coaching schedule look like to move the client to the top right corner of the Hope/Pain Matrix?

2. What are some specifics that you could suggest moving a new client from F1B1 to F3B2 within one month of beginning the Coaching Program?

3. What are the consequences of moving a client to F4B1? To their supporter network, self, and peers they are friends with and/or working within their recovery efforts?

4. Using the Hope/Pain Matrix, what suggestions could you make that might solve the cost, time, and knowledge gaps to fit a typical client's requirements?

Communication During Behavioral Sobriety™ Coaching Sessions

Setting Up Great Communication

In the next segments, we will go over the communication skills required to be an effective coach include the capability to:

1. Pose effective questions.
2. Actively listen without judgment.
3. Provide feedback effectively that provokes thoughtful responses
4. Help the client work through meaningful goals leading to desired outcomes.
5. Hold the client accountable to their goals and promises.

A few well-chosen or poorly-chosen words or posing the right question at just the right moment in a person's life, can transform their views, beliefs, goals and outcomes for the rest of their life.

During your coaching sessions, the roles of sender and receiver constantly shift. As soon as you send a message to your client, your expectation is that they will respond to you. The same happens when they speak. What is often misunderstood about the sender/receiver relationship is that there are no lines of distinction between when you stop sending and begin receiving—and vice versa. In fact, you continue receiving communication from others even when you are sending out messages. Your senses are constantly picking up signals sent – body language, interruptions, etc. - even while you are speaking. When you are listening, you often can't help that your body signals responses through conscious or unconscious body language.

1. If you are sending or receiving a message during a coaching session, you need to make sure that your body language is supporting your intended communication.

2. It also means that your non-verbal communication can stand in the way of effective communication. You may be clear verbally about something, however, the client may not have accurately received the message. Why? Your body language (accompanying the verbal message) didn't lined up with your intent. Example: Delivering a tough message when you are slouching isn't desirable! Stand up straight and/or look serious-minded when you speak about thoughtful issues. The client will see that you mean business!

3. This tells you that it is not just WHAT you say, but HOW you say it (our verbal inflection) that can make a huge difference in your communication to clients.

Client Perception Overrides Reality

Perception is how a person filters reality through their senses. In much communication, perception overrides reality. A client's experiences, beliefs and values provide the building blocks of their specific perception. Their stress level when they hear a message plays a part in how they interpret that communication. Sometimes, you'll shake your head, thinking: *"How could they possibly think that?"* The answer is either:

- They filtered your message through their perception; or
- Your filter and delivery skewed your intent. You thought you said something clearly but because of your filter, something went haywire.

During coaching sessions, it is extremely important to pay attention to the client - what they are *saying and doing* - and to have clarity on the context of the conversation. In relating to the client, you will be able to prepare what to say or do next. Whatever they think of your message, the other person will in turn respond to it - either in a positive or negative fashion.

Pose Effective Questions

Much of what a Recovery Coach does is observational. We watch and listen to client's signals. Much of this observation comes because of asking questions. Gathering information is a basic human activity. People use information to learn, help solve problems, assist in decision making, and to understand each other better. Questioning is the key to gaining more information and confirming what we already know. The bottom line: Without effective questioning techniques, your coaching sessions are bound to be a lot less effective. We already know that if you ask questions when trust is low and/or emotions are high, conversations can go badly.

Ask Questions to:

- **Maintain control of a conversation:** The person asking the questions is typically in control of the conversation. They set the pace, determine the direction, and bring up the topics under examination.
    - "How old were you when you drank more than you should have and didn't remember what you did afterwards?"
    - "What type of friends do you hang out with now since you're in recovery?"
    - "How is your relationship with each of your family members since you've been going to regular meetings?"
- **Explore the person's emotional state:** It's often necessary to make the person aware of their emotional state. Bringing

awareness through questions is a softer, and highly effective way of broaching the 'emotions' subject.

- "I noticed that when you heard Betty speak, that your demeanor changed. What happened?"
- "What upset you in the last five minutes?"
- "How are you feeling today?"
- "How have you been feeling since our last conversation? I know this was setting up to be an emotion-filled week."

- **Obtain Information:** Gathering information provides a window into the client's thinking on a subject. It can tell you what path they're heading down, if they've put adequate (or appropriate) thought into something, or if they are ready to explore other options.

  - "Do you have a plan or know the best way to stay away from the people who tempt you when you go visit family in Cleveland over the holidays?"
  - "When did you first realize you might be in trouble?"

- **Seek clarification and/or reduce misunderstandings:** Perception and filtering skew understanding. Asking clarifying questions is vital to get people on the same page.

  - "Could I take a moment to ask you what you meant when you said that you had never seen someone in such dire straits recover so quickly?"
  - "I thought I heard you say that you were feeling badly that you hadn't spoken to John. Isn't John the guy you were nearly arrested with twice? Isn't he your high school friend who is dealing? What is going through your head about wanting to talk to him?"

- **Express an interest:** You can open up further conversations about a subject if you show interest by asking a follow up question.

- "That's interesting. Can you tell me more about it?"
- "So, you enjoyed working through Step 9? You said it gave you some kind of mental release. Can you tell me more?"

- **Assist someone:** Many people never ask for help, but if asked if they'd accept it, they will.
  - "Can I help you work through that activity?"
  - "Can I provide a bit of insight into what might be going on here?"
  - "Can I help out by walking you through some steps that might clarify things?"
  - "Would it relieve your burden a bit if I just sat and listened?
  - "Can I ease your mind by saying that it's ok? Lots of people go through things like this. Does it make you feel any better knowing that you're not alone in this?"
  - "What might improve your state of mind and how can other people help you?"

- **Encourage Participation:** Coaching sessions can be stressful, and some clients shut down. Questions can help a client open up. **Take care to monitor the client's stress level when posing questions.** Many find answering questions about themselves very stressful. Make certain to watch for signs that the client isn't feeling too uncomfortable, embarrassed or awkward. As your coaching sessions progress and trust goes up, these emotions will most likely lessen.
  - "What about taking a facilitator role in our next group session? I think this will be a good way to work on your communication goals. What do you think?"
  - "I've noticed that you shut down whenever I ask about what happened with your parents. I know this is stressful

to discuss but this is a safe place for those discussions. Do you know that sometimes, by just starting to get things out in the open, they don't seem quite as bad? How can we start the ball rolling on getting this out on the table?"

> Every human being is an artist, a freedom being, called to participate in transforming and reshaping the conditions, structures and thinking that shape and inform our lives.
>
> Joseph Beuys

- **Gain trust or Build Rapport:** People love to have something in common with those they confide in. Asking questions to establish common interests, experiences, work-life, habits, ways of looking at life, locations, or linkages in interests might be an effective gateway to building these.
  - "I didn't know you were from Buffalo, too. When did you leave there? Where did you go to school? Are your family members still in the area?"
  - "I like history, too. What kind of history do you find most fascinating?"
  - "My daughter loves drawing! I think she gets that talent from my dad. Where do you think you got your talent from?"
- **Test knowledge:** Quizzes, examinations, and pointed questions about the grasp a client has on subject matter knowledge is a fundamental in coaching sessions. You cannot effectively move forward in a coaching discussion if you aren't on the same page with a concept, model or theory.

- "Are you familiar with Perceptual Prisms?"
- "Do you know much about Maslow's Pyramid of Motivation?"
- "Have you ever heard of the Love-Hurt-Anger Model?"

- **Inspire deeper thought:** A question may be posed to encourage a client to think about something at a deeper level or to have them contemplate a topic in a new way.
  - "Why do you think it important to stop smoking when you are also giving up weed? Have you thought about the physical act of smoking and how it's linked to both? There's some interesting links between similar physical habits and the risk of relapse."
  - "Learning more about decision making actually makes you better at making decisions. Studies show that reading one or two articles is often enough to change thought processes. Isn't that fascinating?"

- **Get the client 'out of the weeds':** People can get wrapped around the axel and stuck in the weeds if they can't rise above any inconsequential trifling matters, minutia, or get away from the details.

COACHES AREN'T PERFECT, AND CAN JUMP TO CONCLUSIONS

Before we continue, it's important to consider that coaches are human and therefore, are not perfect. We have to allow for the temptation to jump to conclusions. We have to consider that we may be prone to letting assumptions cloud our thinking. *How do we steer clear of doing this?* Instead of closing off dialog, which may prevent important information from surfacing, we can ask more questions that are designed to uncover facts and discover intentions.

As coaches, we always have to remember that a side effect of not asking enough questions is a breakdown of process and that means flawed thinking can enter the coaching sessions. Too few questions being asked might mean there's incomplete analysis. This may result in less than desirable decision-making. During coaching sessions, targeted intention-based questions are important.

Great coaches take the time to figure out how to ask better questions. They slow down and listen. Then they ask follow-up questions for clarification. In this way, the client can learn how to come to better conclusions. Just as important, questions save time. If you haven't asked the appropriate questions in a timely manner, you'll only have to circle back to them later.

Responses to Questions

> Between stimulus and response there is a space.
>
> In that space is our power to choose our response.
>
> In our response lies our growth and our freedom.
>
> - Viktor Frankl

There are a variety of questioning techniques. It stands to reason there must also be a number of ways a client can respond. One of the first discussions we recommend you have with clients is to go over this page. We suggest that you have the client read it, then discuss the various responses and their pros and cons in detail. Specifically view the consequences in the light of recovery efforts, enhancing and/or damaging relationships, and impact the various response have on the client's Self-Talk and decision making.

A CLIENT CAN PROVIDE A RESPONSE THAT IS A/AN:

- **Honest and direct response:** The truth is the ideal answer, especially during coaching sessions.
- **Partially Answering:** Clients may give an incomplete, limited, biased, one-sided, or be selective about which questions or parts of questions they prefer to respond to. Perhaps the client does this to appear 'better' than they think society views them. Maybe this is a pattern of behavior. Possibly the client is embarrassed, ill at ease, proud, humiliated, shy, uncomfortable, nervous, or self-conscious and that is the reason they feel they cannot disclose everything. Whatever the case, a Recovery Coach must probe and get to the bottom of the issue. Full, honest, forthright answers are the goal. Any of the reasons previously listed run counter to recovery efforts. Authentic responses require that the client move forward through their discomfort. In all instances, it requires being:
  - Trustworthy
  - Genuine
  - Realistic
  - Accurate
  - Dependable
  - Reliable
  - Authentic
  - Truthful

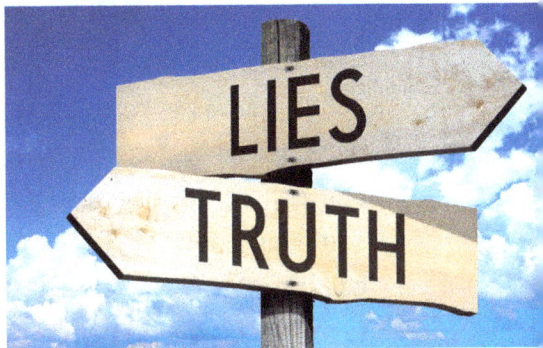

- **Stalling:** Although similar to avoiding answering a question, clients can use stalling when they don't want to respond right now. They'll also use stalling tactics when they need a bit more time to put together an acceptable answer. This isn't always a negative. Sometimes a coach has to allow for this.

- **Misunderstanding/Out of context:** The client may not understand the intent or context of the question. As such, they may respond with words that are disconnected or irrelevant to the question. It may be appropriate to rephrase your question or come at the topic in another way in these cases.

- **Refusal:** The client can refuse to answer, either by remaining silent or by saying, 'I am not answering'.
  - "I'd rather not talk about that."
  - "That's too painful."
  - "Can we move on to something else now?"
  - "Why do we have to go there? I'm really not going to tell you that stuff."

> When someone can't answer a direct question, it's probably because the truth is too painful for you to know, or more likely, too painful for them to admit.

- **Lies that are Technically Truths:** Two forms of lying often occur in coaching sessions. Some people use this strategy because in their minds, they're telling the truth (allowing distorted perception) or not actually lying because they aren't saying something untruthful (willful omission). So, they think they're being honest. Make no mistake, it's all about intention to deceive to make something happen in their favor. People who do this might need an immediate reminder about what it feels like to be on the other side of a lie of omission or paltering. Anyone deceived in this manner will simply think the other person is being just as dishonest as if they lied outright to their faces.

- **Willful Omission:** Lying by omission happens when a person purposefully leaves out important information or fails to correct a misconception in order to hide the truth. Their rationale: "But I didn't lie. I just didn't tell you." Coaching discussion: "Leon, I thought you discussed this matter with your partner, Joseph, last week I assumed you were ok with meeting on Thursday just after lunchtime. You said you liked that time. I just got a text from Joseph asking why I am insisting our meeting happen then. And they're asking why the meeting can't happen early morning before you go to work, or late in the afternoon after you finish work. I blocked off time and rescheduled a few other meetings to accommodate your request. It wasn't my requirement to meet when you wanted. Why would both of us be wondering what happened here?" Leon responds: "Well, I didn't tell Joseph that you made the schedule. When I told him the meeting time, he just assumed. And I didn't tell you that I couldn't meet at any other times, I just said I liked meeting right after lunch. I didn't lie about it at all!" Coaching discussion: "Ok, Leon, that's technically true, but you weren't forthcoming either. The result is that Joseph thinks my scheduling is upsetting your work scheduling and setting the wrong precedent at the office." Do you understand how that might happen when you didn't let either of us into the picture? I think you just wanted to leave work for a break midday. I know so many hours at that pace haven't been good for your stress levels." Joseph probably doesn't know that you used to drink during the day, does he? I get it, but lying by omission to get something accomplished isn't good for your recovery efforts. We agreed on honesty and transparency. Weren't you worried one of us would question this? What are your actions to fix this misunderstanding and get us back on track?"

- **Paltering:** Paltering is a form of deception that happens when a person makes statements that are technically true but are purposely uttered to skew perception or to mislead. When a client is paltering, they know they're giving a false or distorted impression, even if they're telling the truth. "Leon, how far did you get in the 'Book About Me' workbook activities?" Leon palters: "I actually enjoyed reading the section on Self-Talk (which he knows is late in the workbook). I think the activities are very well designed." In this instance, Leon has only skimmed through the workbook and has not completed one single activity! But he is technically not lying. If you find this occurring, ask for verification.

- **Distortion:** Clients may give distorted answers to questions based on their perceptions of social norms, stereotypes, the culture they grew up in, the influences of other people in their life, their experiences, and/or other forms of slanted decision making, prejudices, or biases. Distortion is a bit unlike outright lying because clients may not realize their answers are influenced by thought patterns that are skewed or biased. As an example, clients might not realize they are exaggerating. Exaggeration is a form of distortion. When clients use exaggeration, they are trying to skew perception of who they are or where they came

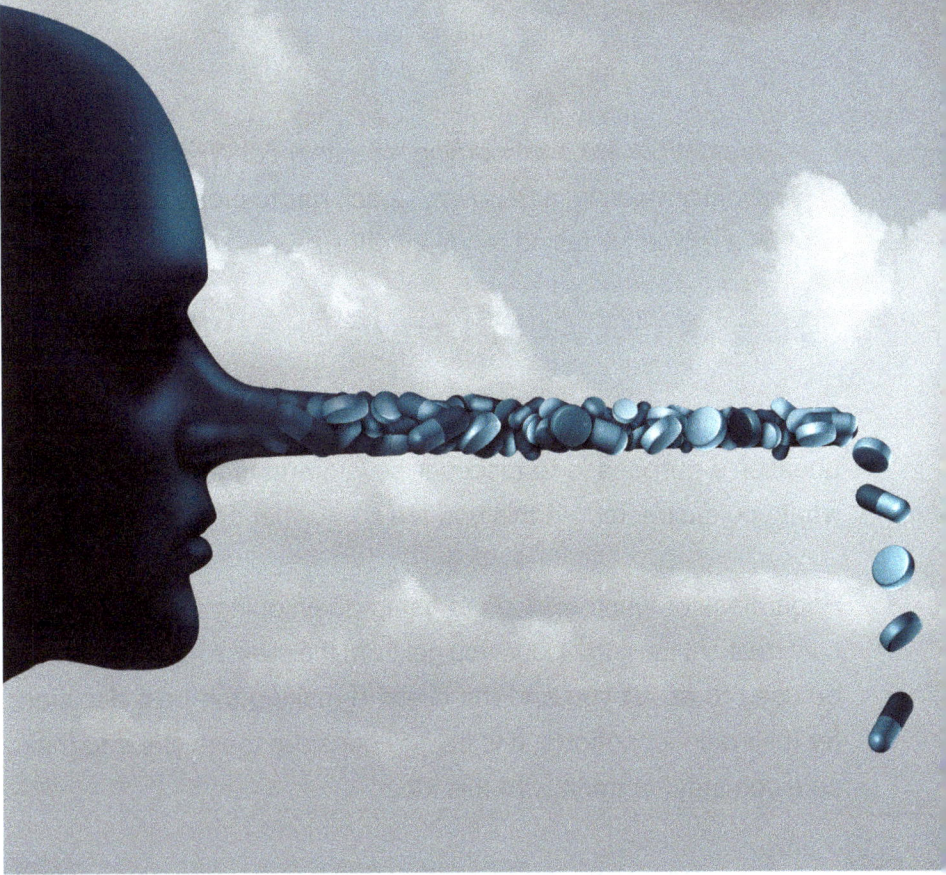

from. Whether they do so to come across as more 'normal' or successful is irrelevant. What is relevant is that they are not being forthright, honest, or authentic. The reasons they are using distortion should be a topic of coaching sessions.

- **Untruth or Lie:** Clients lie for a variety of reasons. A Recovery Coach must anticipate this. The best way to uncover the truth and discover lies is to ask probing questions and maintain a safe and trust-filled environment for your coaching sessions.
- **Avoiding the answer**: When asked a 'difficult or tough question' which probably has an answer that would shed a potential negative on the client, they choose to wiggle out of answering. They make the choice to evade or sidestep the request for truthful information rather than being frank, open,

straightforward, forthcoming, or authentic. When clients try to avoid answering, a Recovery Coach has to probe why. Avoiding is a recipe for failing recovery efforts.

Discovery or Confirmation Questioning

The first consideration when you ask questions is to decide if your question's purpose is to discover new information and to confirm what you suspected. In this you are somewhat of a detective.

Regardless of whether you are using questioning for discovery or confirmation, the knowledge you get from the client's response should be used to assist you and the client in making the best decisions for their recovery efforts. It is best to consider these steps to make sure you stay on track with this ideal:

1. Review new information to effectively deduce value and meaning. Get supplemental insight from as many sources as possible.
2. Reference existing and supplementary facts if available.
3. Establish significance and relevance of new information.
4. Determine how the context of this information changes any prior understandings, promises, or undertakings. Ask: Does this new input change the intentions, meaning or situations.
5. Derive new ways of thinking/different approaches from the information. Figure out the consequences and impacts (if any).
6. Have the client determine if any decisions need to be adjusted or made. Have the client offer suggestions or recommendations from the resulting knowledge.

NEW INFORMATION

When your client provides you with additional knowledge, you have to allow for this information to meld (assimilate) with what you already know. But before you do that, you should confirm the new information is factual, has merit, or is relevant. During coaching sessions, the purpose of any information is to turn what you know into something useful for recovery efforts.

NEW INFORMATION CRITERIA

New information should be viewed as useful for **three general purposes**:

Leads to an increase in understanding.

1. Steers toward a decrease in uncertainty.
2. Can be used for better decision making.

The **litmus test** for new information should be that it is:

1. Accurate and timely,
2. Specific and organized for a purpose,
3. Presented within a context that gives it meaning and relevance.

Information is valuable because it can affect behavior, a decision, or an outcome. A piece of information is considered valueless if, after receiving it, things remain unchanged. For example, if a client is told his/her company's net profit decreased in the past month, he/she may use this information as a reason to become anxious about their future financial stability. During the coaching session, they might decide to spruce up their resume, look at their monthly spending, and/or just keep their finger in the wind looking for other financial changes in the company. In this way, they keep ahead of the game and keep stress in check. The new information in this example propels action. New information without change is a tad above useless. In this example, if the client does nothing, their anxiety will most certainly increase until newer information enters.

> Embrace uncertainty.
>
> The most beautiful pages, chapters and verses of our lives won't be written until much later.

New Information can resolve uncertainty. This is a powerful concept in coaching. If your client is displaying signs of anxiety, new targeted information can lessen their angst. Information is powerful because when people feel confident, they'll tend to act on information sooner than if they are unsure of the facts.

EXAMPLES OF NEW INFORMATION QUESTIONS:

"Joe, do you think it might be good to check on whether what you're thinking is going to happen, is actually true? You appear to be wondering if one or another of your family members will be at Sunday dinner. Why don't you just ask if they will. It's not very productive to spend your time wringing your hands over whether they'll be there or not. If they won't be there, you can rest easy. If they will be there, let's talk through a strategy to get you through the day. Perhaps it might help to put a different spin on this: You did say you wanted to make amends with them. This might be the perfect opportunity, even though you might think it's too soon. How does that sound? Like a logical thing for you to do?"

SEEKING OUT NEW INFORMATION

In the last example, if the company posted profits the next month, the information provides the answer to the questions that have been bouncing around in the client's head about their future at the company. Technically, the uncertainty of any event is measured by its probability of occurrence. The more info a person has about that probability, the better able they are to assess the risk – to themselves and others. The more uncertain an event, the more information is required to resolve uncertainty of that event.

EXAMPLES OF NEW INFORMATION QUESTIONS:

Dana, based on what's come to light, what changes do you think you need to make this week in your communication with your mom?

Alex, now that you know who'll be at the hearing, how do you think you should dress? How do you think you should act? What do you think are some things you should say to help your case? What are some things you should do or say?

CONFIRMING WHAT YOU THOUGHT WAS CORRECT

One of the characteristics of a great Recovery Coach is their skill in distinguishing between facts and assumptions. An assumption is something anticipated to be correct, even without proof. An example: People might make the assumption that you're a nerd if you wear glasses, even though that's not true. In Recovery Coaching sessions, assumptions need confirmation.

Assumptions aren't bad in and of themselves. It's a Recovery Coach's reliance on them that cause problems. Let's face it. There is no way we can possibly know everything about our clients. We actually spend very little time with them in relation to their entire life. Therefore, Recovery Coaches have to make assumptions. This is a natural process of Recovery Coaching; however, you must continually check assumptions against facts and data. Additionally, you should never use an unconfirmed assumption to make a decision.

> The problem with assumptions is we believe they are truth. We assume, then create misunderstandings. We take things personally, then react. We become emotional, then lash out. Unchecked assumptions are poison.
>
> - Hellen Davis

When you start to figure out who the client is, where they came from, what experiences they had, how best to help them in their recovery efforts, you're on the road to making assumptions. It is what it is. Make two columns in your head when putting the pieces together: One for facts and data you've verified, the other for assumptions. Your mantra must be: **Assume, then Confirm!**

Once you label something as an assumption, you have to determine its impact on your client's ability to work the process and follow through with their responsibilities. If you are not sure if something is a fact, it's an assumption until you prove it otherwise. You must ask questions to resolve assumption versus facts. This is often a very tough thing to do. It may take a while and there might be some uncomfortable moments. It might take some digging. But it must be done.

A word of warning: If you don't realize something is an assumption, it will not cross your mind to confirm it. This is dangerous! New and experienced coaches alike will make this mistake until they realize how critical this concept is for their clients. But the reasons may be different. New coaches may not know enough to have a thorough understanding of the recovery environment or a significant understanding of situations their clients might be dealing with. This is also difficult for experienced Recovery Coaches because, "Hey, I've seen it all. I know exactly what this client needs. Been there, done that!"

How to best guard against assumptions clouding your coaching sessions?

Assume everything you know is an assumption! Then, test your assumptions by asking questions to verify information. Continually check yourself. Ask yourself: "How do I know this?" "How have I verified this?" "Where is the source of this information?" "Has anything changed since I first uncovered these facts?"

Don't make assumptions. Find the courage to ask tough questions. Do so with Noble Intent. Communicate clearly, with a good heart. Do everything in your power to avoid misunderstandings. Vow to hold fast to this principle. It will transform your life.

Learn to question with Broad-based Questions, then drill down with Detail-based Questions until the assumptions are confirmed. This leads you to ask better and more meaningful questions as your coaching relationship matures. The more you practice this the better you will become. Remember, the hardest part about unearthing the facts versus what you are guessing to be true is recognizing what assumptions you are making. You cannot make suggestions, walk the client through the process of formulating a recovery plan, or the like, based on guesses. Guesses are precisely what most assumptions are.

AFTER ACTION REVIEW HELPS STOP ASSUMPTIONS NEXT TIME

As a final step, review every client coaching sessions and encounter. To grow as coaches, we must assess our effectiveness. I know this is true: If you rethink your assumptions, if you review your assumptions in terms of how they might have affected coaching outcomes, you'll be all the better for it. None of us like to do this, but it's vital for your growth as a professional. Ask yourself: What assumptions did you base your approach on that were inaccurate or flawed? What could you have done to confirm you have a thorough understanding next time? How will you recognize that type of assumption in the future? Your best defense against assumptions is to be prepared to look at everything you believe to be true in the light of confirmation.

Timing Questions and Responses

Coaches might not consider the importance of timing and timeliness in asking questions. You can pose questions with a 'timing element' to either

- Promote patience and thoughtfulness or
- Propel action and a sense of urgency.

SPEED OF RESPONSE TIME

You can promote a quicker or slower response time from your client.

SLOWER

If the coach doesn't allow the client the appropriate amount of time to provide a thoughtful response, the coach won't get the response that might be most helpful or one that has the depth of thinking necessary. Or, they'll inadvertently prompt a quicker response than the client should give because the coach looks impatient.

-   "Jessie, if you think about this decision a little more, what are some of the things you need to consider that you haven't already thought about?"
-   "Why don't you take an additional five minutes to consider your answer before you throw one out there?"

QUICKER

If the questions don't promote subsequent action-based thinking, the client's recovery efforts may stall.

-   "Jessie, we talked about what decisions you need to make and what actions you should make sure happen before our next coaching session. They look like they were on the tip of your tongue, just ready to come pouring out. What did you decide was the right timing for actually taking action and getting these things off your plate?"
-   "Why don't you just blurt out the first thing that you're thinking about doing? What's right in front of you – inside your head – right now?"

AS A RECOVERY COACH, CONSIDER BOTH TIMING AND TIMELINESS WHEN ASKING QUESTIONS.

THOUGHTFUL QUESTIONS TAKE PATIENCE

When asking questions designed to make the client think, you have to take on the persona of 'patience and openness'. People often answer too quickly, without adequate thoughtfulness. The worst thing you can do when asking a client thoughtful questions is to instill a sense of urgency. Asking questions requires a certain amount of finesse in order to allow the client to feel that being vulnerable is ok, that not having the perfect answer is fine. More important, allowing time and being thoughtful will allow the client to give you a truthful answer, rather than the one they think you want to hear.

ACTION-BASED QUESTIONS PROPEL MOTIVATION

Action-based and decision-making questions stimulate the client to make choices about what to do. These should propel the client forward and instill a sense of urgency and/or motivation. If you want to help your client make the right decisions, you need to study how the timing of your line of questioning people affects recovery efforts. In your coaching sessions, you must ask the questions that really matter to stimulate timely responses and actions.

> An inch of movement, a grain of action, will take you farther than a hundred miles of intentions.

Big Picture versus Details Questioning

The lens that you view a situation through changes the emotional involvement and the stress a client feels during coaching sessions. One of the models in the 'Book About Me' workbook helps with this line of questioning. Have a look at the section with the Bull's Eye of Motivation.

You'll remember that this model relies on the fact that the client will be more motivated and/or emotional the closer to the center of the bull's eye than they would if they were thinking in terms of the outer

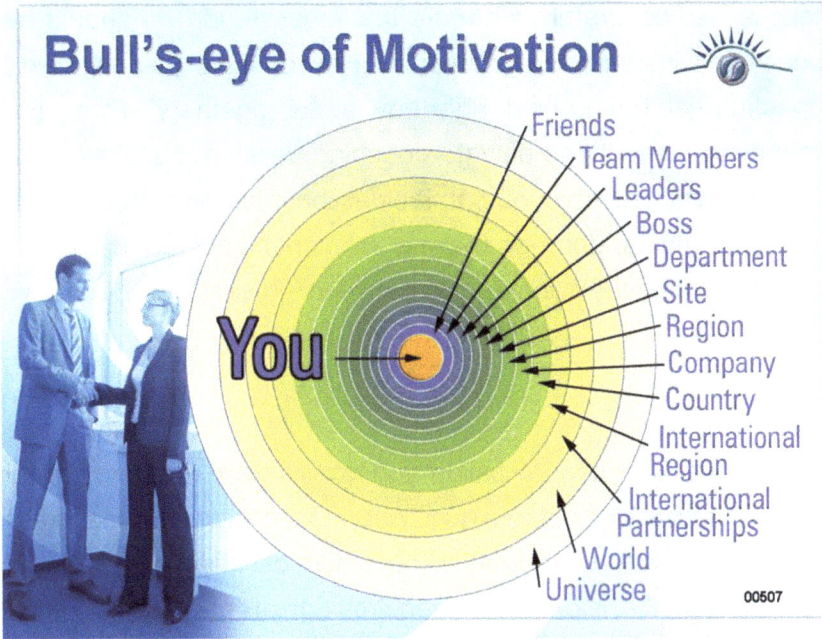

Bull's-eye of Motivation

Friends
Team Members
Leaders
Boss
Department
Site
Region
Company
Country
International Region
International Partnerships
World
Universe

You

00507

rings. The outer rings are the 'Bigger Picture'. The questions that address the inner ring topics typically have detail and impact more relevant to the client.

BIG PICTURE QUESTIONS

Big Picture Questions are designed to look at things from the 30,000-foot level. Asking them helps the client 'zoom out'.

Being too immersed in an immediate problem or issue often makes it harder to see the overall context behind it. Examples of Big Picture Questions: "Taking a step back, what are the larger issues for your recovery efforts?" or "Are we even addressing the right question with this issue? Shouldn't we step back and look at it from a higher level before making any important decisions?" or "Instead of talking about these issues separately, what are the larger trends we should be concerned with regarding your habits? How do the bigger negatively impacting habits you have right now all tie together?" These Big Picture-type questions elevate coaching session discussions to a higher level whereby you can look at the interconnectedness of behaviors, habits, decision making, relationships, etc. The goal is to best examine the connections between individual problems.

DETAIL QUESTIONS

Asking Detail Questions will allow you to do a deep dive into critical areas. Without asking detailed questions, the client may never address the unique behaviors that have a.) held them back and b.) will propel them forward. Decision making requires rigor. Rigor requires detail. It's that simple. The thing to be aware of is that many clients don't like going into detail because it's uncomfortable. Ok. Own this: Your job is to go there (where they don't want to go, have avoided in the past, is too painful, is too hard, will hold them accountable, etc.) by asking detailed questions so they can drill down to what they need to do. That's your responsibility as a Recovery Coach.

> **Detail Questions:** "Now that we've had a look from the 30,000-foot level, we can start to drill down to some of the things that you talked about changing. Let's begin with stimulation that is holding you back form sleeping at night. Then we'll talk about the consequences – short and long term – of fatigue and staying up too late. Let's break it down: What specifically is it that could be causing you to stay awake until the wee hours of the morning?"

Response: I used to drink coffee in the late afternoon, but it didn't affect me like it does now. I guess it's because at night I'd drink. Now that I'm not drinking, I think my system is overly stimulated by the caffeine. There's nothing bringing me down anymore."

Detail Questions: "Ok, I get that. What do you think you can do to avoid caffeine late in the day or do something else to counterbalance its effects?"

Response: "Well, I can stop after 4 pm. That's got to help! Also, I can drink lots more water to dilute it if I do take a cup later in the day. Those two things should help a bit. Also, I can go for a walk and get my juices flowing so that I'll be tired in the evening."

Close out for accountability: "Great, let's put those on the list for this week and circle back about what worked and what didn't next week. Good idea?"

Structuring a Series of Questions

Now that you know a few questioning techniques, let's continue by learning how to string different kinds of questions together. In coaching sessions, it's often the case that you have to ask a series of questions to get to the bottom of the matter, to the root cause. In Recovery Coaching, clients are sometimes adept at 'dodging'. A series of questions can stop them from avoiding the issue and will get them to start discussing what's at the heart of the matter.

Make no mistake, it may take asking a large number of questions to get the client to open up about things they'd prefer not discussing. In these situations, if you know you're going to talk about uncomfortable subjects, it's usually a good idea to tell your client that you're going to start a series of questions that are designed to drill down until the issues are on the table. This gives the client Fair Warning of what's to come.

The definition of giving 'Fair Warning' is to let someone know you are going to do something before you do it. In order to be classified as Fair Warning, you need to give the person adequate forewarning or notice of what you are going to do. The key word is 'adequate'. As an example, if a surgeon is going to perform an elective procedure, the patient should be given Fair Warning about what will happen, including how they might best prepare for a successful outcome. The timeframe for Fair Warning of the impacts should be 24 hours to a few weeks. If a football player is going to set up a play, Fair Warning for their teammates might be between 1 and 5 seconds before the action takes place. In coaching sessions, the Recovery Coach determines adequate Fair Warning. Break the phrase down to determine what you and the client might think is 'Fair', then give warning about what's coming. Then, follow through in the timeframe you stated.

HERE ARE SOME SUGGESTIONS:

Fair Warning in the coming days:

"Harold, in our next session, we're going to start delving into communication. I am giving you Fair Warning that I'll be asking some pointed questions about your history of angry outbursts. We've only brushed on these in past sessions, but I think you're ready for a deeper dive. If you can prepare for this by thinking through some past examples that you might feel ok talking through, no matter how explosive they were, that would be great. I just wanted to tell you this is coming up and that you'll get through it just fine. We'll use the examples to go through the models in the 'Book About Me' workbook. They'll form the basis for learning Anger Management techniques and exploring your Self-Talk.

Fair Warning in the coming moments:

"Judy, I just heard you say something contrary to what you told me just 20 minutes ago. I am giving you Fair Warning that we are going to circle back and fact-check in a moment. I suggest you think through what I'm saying for the next few moments. (Silence) Ok, now let me ask you a couple of tough questions. I expect you won't like this conversation, but we have to delve into what's going on here."

> This technique of giving the client Fair Warning' is powerful for two reasons:
> 1. It provides permission for you to begin.
> 2. It gives the client permission to feel the discomfort you and they know is inevitable.

Informing of intent to drill down usually makes the process go a lot smoother. Provide any background information or model that you would like to discuss at the beginning of the drill down for even better results.

Prior to starting the series of questions, make sure you go into the reasons why the drill down is important for their recovery efforts. By doing this, the client usually is more open to a long series of questions. Also, remember that many of the questions you are supposed to ask probably would seem overly intrusive in any other situation. Coaching sessions are supposed to be where the client gets asked tough questions. Remind them this is part of the process and let them have a little time out for a few minutes if stress levels get too high. And remind yourself: It is acceptable for you to be asking them and why this is critical to their success.

Heads Up to Tough Questions

Another way you can lower the client's stress is to give them a heads up about the type of questions that are likely to come up. Example, "Susan, in order to help you with building trust with your family, it will be vital for me to ask you about that straw that broke the camel's back – as you said it was the event that brought everything crashing down, literally. Can you tell me about your emotions, health, state of mind, and the circumstances that led up to the accident? After

we talk about those, I am going to ask you a series of questions about what has changed in the last six months since the accident. Ok? Some of these are going to be hard for you but we need to get through them all. Are you ready to start?"

Using Silence During Questioning

Using silence after delivering questions has a powerful impact. Pausing and waiting for the client's response can help to emphasize important points. Being quiet can give the client a few moments to gather their thoughts before responding. When you start your coaching sessions, let the client know that it's ok to think before they respond. In fact, this is desirable! One of the things you hope will come from coaching sessions is that the client will learn to think before speaking. It's a skill that many need to learn.

- Training yourself, as a Recovery Coach, to be quiet after asking a question has a few benefits. It can prevent you from asking another question, potentially destroying the impact of the first question. If you keep talking after asking a question, it can confuse the client. You must avoid doing this.

- Silence is also good if the response the client gives isn't detailed enough. If you don't speak, they most likely will.
- Pausing again after an initial response can encourage the respondent to continue with their answer in more detail. Pauses of less than three seconds have been proven to be less effective.

Broad-Brush or Laser-like Questions

Many people never consider that different types of questions can lead to different outcomes. You can steer a conversation one way or another by asking the right kinds of questions, or the wrong questions. You can broaden the aperture of the topic, expanding the view of the issue, topic or problem you are focusing on by asking *Broad-Brush Questions that stimulate general answers*. Or you can narrow the focus and ask *Laser-Like Questions* that require *detail-focused answers*.

Tandem Follow Up Questions

Tandem Follow Up Questions are posed to bridge onto related areas that the client might not want to discuss, but should. These can be either Broad-Brush or Laser-like. Examples: "How would this concept of listening before judging apply in a different context, perhaps something like building up your relationship with your son again?" or "What are two other ways, beside directly helping yourself inside your head, that you can use the Self-Talk Chart this week to communicate better?" Another example, asking "How would these insights apply in your peer group meetings?" during one-on-one coaching sessions can open the client's mind to using the techniques they are learning in other environments outside of the 'safe zone' of your coaching sessions. Often, a person's natural narrow focus on only what's in front of them or an immediate task will hinder them from probing about related topics that should be explored. By asking more Tandem Follow Up Questions, the coaching sessions become richer and broader. This means you can reach into other areas of the client's life more easily. Addiction touches nearly every aspect of a client's life, so this is an important consideration.

HERE ARE SOME SUGGESTIONS:

1. What would it look like if you were entirely successful in your recovery efforts?
   a. **Tandem Follow up:** What would you see if you popped into a time machine and there it was, you maintained your recovery for 30 years?
      - Why do you want that to be your long-term future?
   b. **Detail Follow up:** Why do you want that in the short-term for your kids?
      - Why do you want that for your health?
2. In six months, if things were going exactly the way you want, what would you see?
   a. **Tandem Follow up:** What would be your next goal after you achieve your current one?
      - Why?
   b. **Broad-brush Follow Up:** What would you do if you had unlimited resources in the next six months?
   c. **Detail Follow up:** What about it is so important to you that you would defend it at all costs in the next six months?
3. **Detail Follow up:** What would be the precise impacts on you (and others) if things don't change right now?

a. **Broad-brush Follow up:** What are some things that you can accomplish that doesn't depend on others?

b. **Detail Follow up:** What is your current biggest problem or challenge?

- **Narrow then Broad Approach Follow up:** If this weren't a problem, what would be your biggest problem?

- What is working well?

- What has contributed to your success so far?

4. **Detail Follow up:** How exactly might your unwillingness to set and live by the boundaries you need get in your way?

a. What about boundaries might keep you from getting where you want to go?

b. What obstacles have you faced when you tried to set and enforce boundaries on yourself, what did you do, and what did you learn?

c. What particular obstacles do you expect to face when you are setting boundaries for you and others for your recovery efforts in the next two weeks?

- How specifically do you plan to approach them?

- What particular communication do you think needs to happen?

- Who will be your biggest supporters?

- Who will be the people who will not get on board as easily?

d. What resources do you have access to help with the boundaries you have to set?

e. What are your biggest mistakes and challenges in trying to hold yourself to boundaries and what did you learn from them?

5. If a friend were in your shoes, what particular individual advice would you give them about what they should be concentrating on?

   a. **Follow up:** How can you use your answer to help yourself?

6. What is one step you could take right now that would indicate you were moving forward?

   a. **Follow up:** How would you suggest I help you hold yourself accountable?

      - What are the things you least like about accountability?

7. Are there any important questions that have not been asked?

   a. **Follow up:** Have you ever found yourself avoiding answering questions or dealing with issues?

Planning a Broad then Narrow Questioning Approach

You will find that most clients don't like to discuss touchy or negative topics until they get comfortable. If you start with Broad-Brush Questions then drill down further into the issue by asking a series of Laser-Like Questions, you might find your client opening up more to you, and with less stress.

HERE ARE SOME SUGGESTIONS:

Broad-Brush Question: "You said you went to three meetings this week, at two different locations? How did that go?"

Response: "Great, I was happy that I made it to them all and got the chance to meet a couple of great people."

Broad-Brush Question: "In our last conversation, you were worried about going to the Main Street meeting. Is that one of the ones you went to this week?"

Response: "Yes, that's true. I was anxious."

Laser-Like Questions: "What specifically happened that made you feel better about it?

Response: I walked in the door and Sandy came up and greeted me. I needed to see a friendly face."

Laser-Like Questions: "That's great but why did you think you needed that?"

Response: "The last time I went there I was embarrassed because I gave one of the guys a hard time and I got called out for being rude."

Laser-Like Questions: "That's interesting, John. Why didn't you bring up the real reason at our last session?"

Response: "I didn't want to say anything because we just went over Anger Management the week before and I failed the test that same night!"

Laser-Like Questions: "John, this process takes time. No one, especially me, expects you to be perfect. What I do expect is that you try and learn from things as you go along. As long as the impact of what you did caused you to get better for next time, I'm good with that. And you should be too. Was there anything else about this that you might want to tell me, knowing this is a safe place and I'm not judging you at all?"

Response: "Actually, now that you know all this, I can tell you that I am a little proud of myself! I went up to that guy and said 'sorry'. I told him I was in a bad place and that I shouldn't have taken it out on him. He thanked me and shook my hand. I was really worried about it when I promised to go there in our last coaching session. But I didn't have the guts to bring it up. I did a stand-up thing that

I wouldn't have done before. I took responsibility and tried to make amends. It felt good!"

Laser-Like Questions: "All-in-all, you did great. I'm really proud of you for stepping up and taking on what you did and making it a lot better for you and everyone else, too. Is there anything at all that you'll do differently next time?"

Response: "Well, for a start, I was kicking myself that we didn't talk about it. I think if I had rehearsed what I was going to say, I would have done an even better job. I would have appreciated your listening ear and maybe some suggestions on how to make it better. I felt I hashed it up a bit. You would have laughed. I started with 'Do you remember me? I thought the guy was going to faint. I think he thought I was going to get into it with him instead of apologizing. I'll tell you, he looked worried! Good thing Sandy was standing right next to me and smoothed the beginning part over quickly! After that it was all good."

Tandem Follow Up Question: "John, well done on that one! It was smart to include Sandy. Along that note, do you think it might be good to include a sympathetic sibling in your feelings about Thanksgiving, or perhaps go with one to Thanksgiving with your family? I know that you've really been worrying about that for a while now. We haven't been able to lessen your anxiety over this even after a good few chats. Maybe a similar approach that you used for the Main Street meeting would help? What do you think of that?"

Response: "I think that if you would have said that last coaching session, I would have said 'no way'. But now, I think it might be something to talk over. I shouldn't exclude it like I have before."

Ask a Question to Discover Intention

Knowledge is having the answer.

Intelligence is asking the right question.

The reasons why a question is asked is called 'the intention'. Seeking clarification and understanding of the client's intentions might help you gain insight into why the client is behaving in a certain manner. If you step back and challenge your basic assumptions and/or affirm your understanding, you'll be a better Recovery Coach. You must do this if only to feel more confident in your conclusions.

In many instances, Recovery Coaches request clarification about what a client just said about a topic. *The intention is to gather information to better understand the context and content of the client's message.*

A Recovery Coach may prompt clients to share more information in the moment about thoughts, behaviors, actions, and or feelings. *The intention is to openly discuss what the client is going through in their mind.*

Recovery Coaches should always start a coaching session by asking for or confirming some basic information about what happened with their clients since the last time they spoke. *The intention for the questions is to tie up loose ends, bring the client back to where* the last session left off, and to start the ball rolling on this session without losing continuity.

Coaches ask follow-up questions after assignments, milestones, or tasks were due. *The intention is to assess what the client thought of the assignments. Another intention might be to ascertain the motivational components associated with these. Did the client like them? Or did they find them boring, ineffectual, or uninspiring? Were they too simple or complex?*

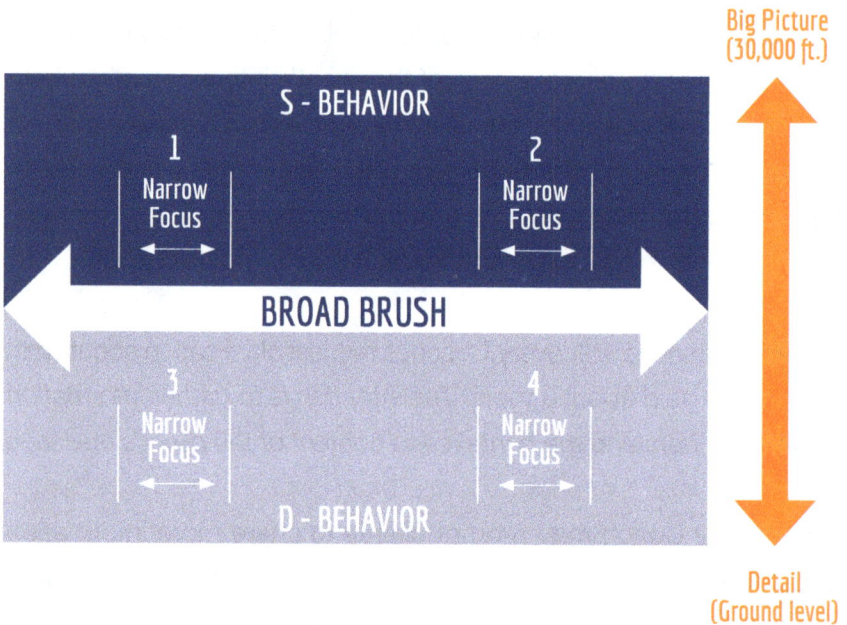

Four Questioning Techniques

Questioning is the art of organizing your thinking around what you don't know.

You can be intentional by using one of four different questioning techniques:

1. Closed
   b. yes/no
   c. information specifics
2. Opened-ended
3. Leading
4. Options and the 'Illusion of Choice'

1.A. CLOSED QUESTIONS: YES/NO

The simplest form of questioning is the Yes/No question. As its name suggests, the answer expected is either yes or no.

Yes/No Questions can be a great way to:

- Check accountability: Did you complete all the activities in the 'Values' section of the 'Book About Me' workbook?
- Figure out the boundaries a client wants/needs for their recovery efforts: Do you think that deleting all the names of people who are not conducive to your recovery efforts from your phone and contacts list is a good idea?

- Ascertain what appropriate next steps might be: Do you want to start learning how to change your xxx habits this week?

Sometimes this question is answered with a modifier or 'hedge'. If this is the case, the answer might be perhaps, maybe, or sometimes (or the like). In coaching sessions, when the client doesn't answer either yes or no, you must delve deeper.

1.B. CLOSED QUESTIONS: DATA/SPECIFICS

Closed Data/specifics Questions look for a specific and quantifiable response other than a Yes or No. They are most often posed to gather information and to negotiate limitations or boundaries.

Closed Data/specifics Questions can be a great way to:

- Lock down information: What time will you be available on Tuesday?
- Quantify particulars: You said that you wanted to complete the 'Habits' section in the 'Book About Me' workbook by what specific date?
- Negotiate limits and boundaries: What would an acceptable method for communicating with you be? Do you prefer text, email, or phone call to set appointments? What times are best for contacting you? Are there any limits on when I can text or call?
- Gather details: How many times did you attend a meeting last week?

2. OPEN-ENDED QUESTIONS

As a Behavioral Sobriety™ Coach, it's very important to have an inventory of powerful open-ended questions. Opened-ended questions are answered by more than a simple yes or no. Open-ended can be one of your most powerful coaching tools. In fact, the 'Book About Me' workbook contains many opened-ended questions in its activities.

By using open-ended questions on a consistent basis, you can help your client 'program the way they respond to themselves internally', visualizing a result, or putting emotional involvement into play. As a Behavioral Sobriety™ Coach, your focus and your questions determine to a large extent the direction the coaching session will go. The 'Book About Me' workbook goes into detail about how important the subconscious mind is in recovery efforts.

One of the best ways to tap into its power is to employ open-ended questions. Please note that opened-ended questions are a tool, but they are not the only questioning tool. There are times when leading questions, yes/no questions, etc. are appropriate. Remember this: Where the subconscious leads the conscious mind follows. The conscious mind is the place where 'actions are decided and acted on'.

So how exactly does this process work? When our subconscious mulls over questions, it kicks into gear in trying to answer or respond. If the question requires a 'yes' or 'no' answer. It shuts itself off thinking "I'm done." When it hears opened-ended questions, it can't get to 'done' easily. Answering requires a more thoughtful response and deeper way of thinking. By posing the appropriate question during your coaching sessions, you can make sure that your client is more thoughtful. You can stage your questions to illicit various responses. These can help the client become motivated, energetic, remorseful, talkative, angry, open to debate, etc. The key to a great coaching session is posing the appropriate questions to invoke appropriate response.

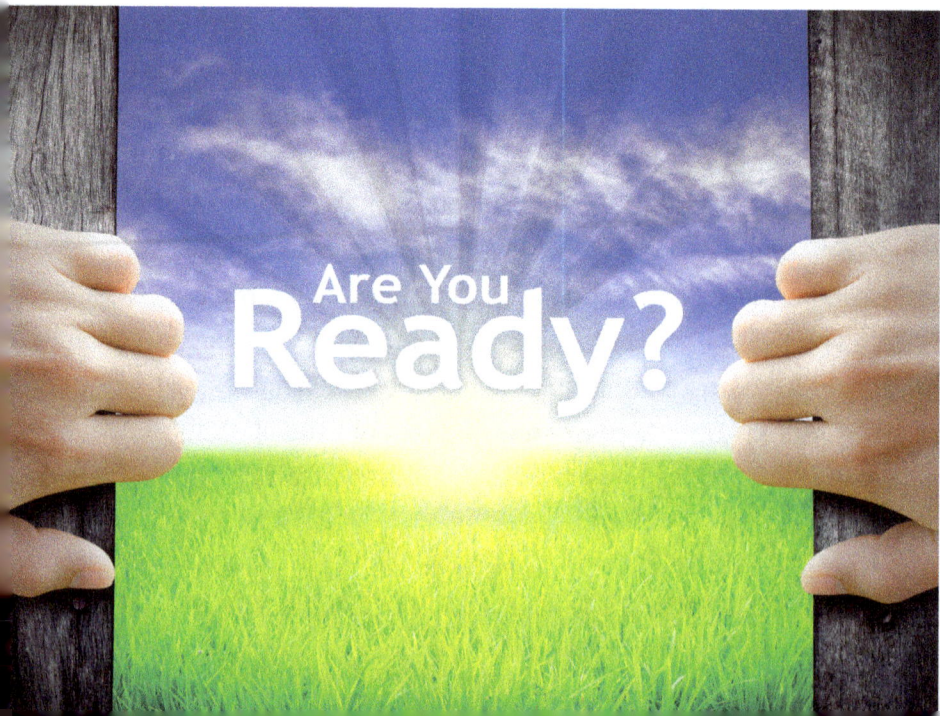

WHAT DO OPENED-ENDED QUESTIONS DO?

- They can help you establish rapport, trust, and credibility. *How did today's session help you?*
- They make it easier to gather information. *You said you were unhappy on Monday, what happened to cause that?*
- They help your client open-up. *Can you tell me more about that? How did that make you respond?*
- They help you in digging deeper, perhaps to qualify what you've heard. *You said you went to a meeting three times last week. Can you tell me about each and what you learned?*
- Opened-ended questions help the client become directly involved in the coaching session's discussion. *You seem a bit distracted/stressed. What is creating that today?*

HOW DO YOU LAUNCH OPENED-ENDED QUESTIONS?

Ask the question and let your client respond.

DO NOT interrupt.

DO NOT prompt.

DO NOT lead. (Note: A leading question pressures, prods for, or encourages a preconceived or desired answer. Example: Why don't you get more excited about this activity? Can you see how beneficial it is for you? Assumes client isn't excited. This question calls the client out about their level of emotions and is judgmental regarding this.)

DO be quiet.

DO be respectful.

DO be patient.

OPENED-ENDED QUESTIONS (SAMPLES)

- What other concerns, opportunities and/or topics should we discuss today?
- Can you help me understand that a little better?
- What exactly does that mean? Can you give me a bit more insight into your thinking on this?
- How did that work out and what would you change for now?
- What challenges does that boundary create?
- What challenges has that kind of boundary created in the past? Let's get specific for you/those impacted?
- What are the best things about _____?
- With whom have you had success with boundaries in the past?
- With whom have you had difficulties with boundaries in the past?
- What prompted you to act like that given the situation?
- What made you want to investigate this more?
- What are your expectations/requirements for this solution to be right for you?
- What is it that you'd like to see yourself accomplish in the next day/three days/week/month/year/3 years?
- What process did you go through to determine your current recovery needs so far/right now?
- How do you see this unfolding if you do have that conversation?

OPEN-ENDED QUESTIONS CAN HELP CLARIFY

When you ask clarifying questions to better understand what has been said, your client will appreciate it. Please remember that often people speak past one another. Asking illuminating questions can help uncover the real intent behind what is said. Have you ever had someone ask a question that, if you probed a little, you might uncover the actual intention? Digging deeper can provide better understanding and help us understand the client better. It can also lead us toward even better and more relevant follow-up questions. "That's interesting! Can you tell me more about that?" and/or "Why did you think that when you…." or "That response makes me ask why…?" In general conversations between people, they rarely dig deeper to ask 'uncovering questions' for fear of being rude, of prying, or appearing overly curious or nosey. The result is they tend to make assumptions and complete any missing parts themselves.

3. LEADING QUESTIONS OR 'SUGGESTIVE INTERROGATION'

Leading question or suggestive interrogation is a question that hints at the answer the coach is looking for from the client. The problem with leading or suggestive questions is that clients will often 'tell you what you want to hear'. So, this form of questioning must bear this in mind. The question itself contains the information the coach wants the client to confirm.

Leading questions do have a benefit in that you can use them to watch a client's reaction. "In our last coaching session, you said that you would call two people and reach out to break the ice. Did you find out that your mom liked that you took the time to call her?"

The risk is that if the mom didn't like it at all, the client will be less forthcoming than had the Recovery Coach asked an opened-ended question: "How did your call with your mom go?"

However, if you do want to get a positive response or reduce fear, a leading question may be the best tactic. What's the worst that can happen? You don't think your mom will immediately bite your head off, do you?" Depending on the circumstances, leading questions can be objectionable or appropriate. Additionally, leading questions may often be answerable with a yes or no *("You had a great conversation with your mom?")*, or they can be opened-ended questions *("How did your great conversation with your mom go?")*.

HOW TO AVOID LEADING QUESTIONS

Here are some samples of leading questions and how to avoid them:

Do you have any problems with your facility/counselor/spouse/boss? (Assumes the client is experiencing problems and prompts a response detailing those problems.)

Did you enjoy your assignment? Wasn't it fantastic?

Including the word fantastic can lead respondents.

A neutral question would be: What did you think of the activity? What did you learn about yourself?

If you were to go to a treatment facility, such as RecoveryAlps, Happy Valley, or YouCanDoIt, where would you like to book into?

By giving examples within the question, you're providing answers, swaying the thoughts of the client. If you'd like more thoughtful answers don't give any leading examples. If you'd like clients to narrow down a list of options, ask them to choose their top 1 or 3.

"Do you agree that Bayside should be your home meeting room?" (Do you agree makes this a leading question, meaning a 'Yes' from the client would be more likely.)

To adjust for this, change the question to: 'Should you consider Bayside when you look for a home meeting room for yourself?"

Below, we'll examine how to avoid leading questions during your coaching sessions. Please note that the third question will get you the most reliable response, because each of the first two questions are leading questions. Leading means that the phrasing of the question itself **includes or implies the desired answer**.

Question 1: "I suspect you were having difficulty with the activity in the 'Book About Me' workbook. What happened?"

Problem: The coach may not be an accurate representation of the client's experience. The coach may anticipate the client had difficulty but that's not what happened at all! The client may have found the activity easy, insightful, or a host of other experiences.

Question 2: "Why did you have difficulty with the activity?"

Problem: Again, this question implies the answer and assumes that client had difficulty. It is a blunt leading question which the client may find objectionable.

Question 3: *"What was easy, challenging, exciting, or difficult about getting to the heart of the activity?"*

This opened-ended question steers the client to the topic of interest (the activity) without suggesting what the experience may have been like for them. It also puts forth a variety of possible responses with none being in command. The client can say pick one or add to the list, without disagreeing with the client. Here the Recovery Coach offers a 'general frame' for the topic of the question, rather than suggesting a response (leading).

LEADING USING RHETORICAL QUESTIONS

The purpose of rhetoric, or the art of influencing, persuading and convincing, is to speak or write in a way where your point is clear without having to say something directly. Rhetorical questions are the inquiring way of making a point using something that is obvious. Rhetorical questions are often humorous and don't require an answer. But we suggest that you avoid them during coaching sessions. Please remember that a rhetorical question is a question that is used to make a point, rather than to actually get an answer. You should want to open dialogue, not shut it down.

Rhetorical questions are:

1. things that are obvious or verifiably true (and most of the general populous would agree to the point) or
2. things that are impossible or meant as a metaphor.

Often rhetorical question are used to challenge or provoke a response by pointing out something that is quite obvious to drive home your point. Professors, teachers, politicians, lecturers, religious leaders, and others use rhetorical questions to help keep attention of their audiences. 'Who wouldn't like to win the lottery?', is not a question that requires a direct response. Why do rhetorical questions influence us? The human brain is programmed to answer any question it is asked. This is true even if the speaker doesn't wait for a response. It the answer is obvious; the responder and speaker are generally in agreement.

Example:

*   You didn't possibly think I would say yes or agree to that did you?
*   There is no point, is there?
*   Are you kidding me?
*   Is there anyone smarter than you?
*   Can we do better next time?
*   Do you want to be a success in this world?
*   Is this supposed to be some kind of a joke?
*   Do you want to be a big failure for the rest of your life?

Rhetorical questions are often used by speakers in presentations to get the audience to think – rhetorical questions are, by design, used to promote thought. Rhetorical questions can make people think along the same lines. They can effectively unite the asker and responder. Example: "No one wakes up and says: "I want to be an addict, do they? No one says they want to be hooked on pain pills, do they?" That's a possible benefit for using them; but do so judiciously. Why? Because the pitfalls can far outweigh any benefits. Another word of caution: Rhetorical questions can seem sarcastic. There is no place for sarcasm in Recovery Coaching.

WHY SHOULD YOU AVOID RHETORICAL QUESTIONS DURING COACHING SESSIONS?

Asking rhetorical questions might make the client feel like foolish. These types of questions can also come across as very rude. If you ask a rhetorical question regarding a person's behavior, the client would know right away that you are very unhappy about what they are doing. But since the question doesn't promote a response, it isn't a terribly healthy way to bring up a point about the client's negative or destructive behaviors. Best advice: Avoid asking negative rhetorical questions.

Here are some negative examples:

- *Don't you think that you should have known what would happen?*
- *Can't you do anything that you promised during our coaching sessions?*
- *Would you like to say that a little bit louder so that I know you're serious this time?*

As you can imagine, even if all of these are true, the client could feel that they are being attacked. From a historical standpoint, most people will only use rhetorical questions when they are terribly frustrated and will probably want/need to apologize about it later.

4. OPTIONS AND THE 'ILLUSION OF CHOICE'

As a coach, you'll soon realize that clients often need help coming up with options to move forward in their recovery efforts. They just don't know what might work for them. As a Behavioral Sobriety™ Coach, you NEVER want to direct. You should ALWAYS provide options. The key is to provide options that work with the client's individual goals, value system, and resources, where either choice is basically the same (and leads to your outcome) but is worded differently. One way to do this effectively is to use the fourth questioning method: Options and the Illusion of Choice.

WHY IS IT CALLED THE ILLUSION OF CHOICE?

Because this method is designed to propel the client forward toward any choice other than what they are currently doing. Movement forward by providing options is highly effective in getting 'stalled' clients to take action that help their recovery efforts. The specific goal when using a double bind is to get the client to think about making decisions that align with a desired outcome. To produce an effective Options Question, you use two 'commands' or 'action statements' that would have basically the same outcome (moving the influencing process forward) in a questioning method.

By using at least two alternatives within an Options Question during your coaching sessions you can:

- Create the illusion of choice (The client will pick one and move forward.)
- Utilize that illusion to install suggestion (The client doesn't know which way to go and you provide suggestions/options.)
- Hide your suggestion so that it is unrecognizable (By using a question, you are not directing. Therefore, the client might 'own it' without as much energy, time and emotional expenditure.)

THE OPTIONS QUESTION

An Options Question is a structure that subtly influences the client by giving them the **illusion of choice**. The options/suggestions you provide inside the question allow the client to make a decision on which option might be best. The question's suggestions ideally will propel recovery efforts forward. The differences in the options might simply be:

- the time frame in which the client's goal will be met,
- the specifics of how the process of meeting the goal will come about,
- how the details of deal will be structured,
- which day you will meet,
- the time/s of day that is best, etc.

> The bottom line: You get someone to do what you want them to do by giving them two options – and you don't really care which one they choose! You get closer to your goal – they feel that they are in control.

Note: During the coaching session, you are not necessarily looking for an immediate answer to the question. You can assume that the person will consent to any of the options and move forward. Sometimes it's best not to wait for a response, and simply assume they'll make the correct choice. You can circle back to it later to make sure they thought about it and decided what they'll do. Often, it's a much better coaching tactic to use your senses (observing, listening, and feeling) to gauge whether a person is moving forward or not.

GUIDELINES FOR THE EFFECTIVE USE OF OPTIONS QUESTIONS

- Make sure the client trusts you.
- Progress from **mental to physical**. Always try to bind a person's **thoughts** first, then work progressively towards binding

physical movement. If you want them to do something, give some alternatives about the thinking behind that before they actually go do it! Plan, then do!

- You must deliver the double bind **effectively and meaningfully**, with the best of intentions without leading the client towards one or the other. Remember, all the options are just fine if the client picks one and moves forward!

- From the chart below, you'll see that it really doesn't matter which option your client picks from the pairings. Either choice will move them forward.

PAIRING COMBINATIONS FOR DOUBLE BINDS	
Learn to let go and support this process	Continue with your recovery efforts by learning more about how to trust the process
Be open	Be receptive
Be interested	Get excited
Trust me	Believe me
Make it a habit	Use it daily
Work it into this month's budget	Set it up to start paying that debt next month
Get enthusiastic in a few minutes	Build up your excitement as you succeed one step at a time
Invest meaningful time with your friends and family	Get on board with reconnecting with your family
Consider the cost savings	Let it positively impact your bottom line
Agree to new ways of acting	Think about how to create new habits
Recognize accomplishments	Look at personal wins
Apply it	Use it
Consider alternatives	Choose an option
Make an appointment	Sit down over lunch/coffee
Accept it as fact	Take it as truth
Use this knowledge daily	Integrate it into your daily life
Invest in your future right away	Understand how you can use this to help your recovery efforts after you figure out a few more details of your plan
Get excited immediately	Think about how happy this will make you

EXAMPLES

The illusion of choice happens during communication a lot more than you think! Look at these historical sentences. We've underlined all the options in each statement.

When will a man discover that he is the master-gardener of his soul, **sooner or later?** *(Does it really matter when this enlightenment occurs?)*

Ask ourselves this: We must all **hang together or** assuredly we shall all **hang separately**?

- BENJAMIN FRANKLIN, to the other signers of the Declaration of Independence

Will I **accept** if nominated **or serve** if selected? No!

- WILLIAM TECUMSEH SHERMAN, message to the Republican National Convention

HEALTH AND RECOVERY

I know you've been thinking about losing weight and starting an exercise program now that you're feeling better. You've talked about it for months. This might make you feel even better in general. It's clearly been bothering you so today we'll set some time aside to discuss this. Bottom line: If you've already decided this is something you want to do, you must decide how and when to start. The choices of 'how' aren't completely clear yet. And we don't know which will work for you. There are lots of ways to go about this. Have you started the research yet? **Count calories and walk a couple times a week** or just **reduce food portions and climb the stair**s at work instead of using the elevator? Can you think of some more that might work for you as a starting point? How about coming up with some benefits to your overall recovery efforts and tap into this as motivation, too?

COMMUNICATION AND RECOVERY

So far, you have been learning different ways to speak to people to make it easier for them to understand what you're going through right now. As you continue to learn to use the natural strengths in your behavior pattern, do you think that you will find thinking about them and using your strengths as an approach will help you? Finding a way to have critical conversation is important to your recovery efforts. How do you think you'll **do this in your family life in general** or to **enable you to be a more thoughtful husband and father**?

HEALTH AND WELL-BEING

Mike, you can either **count calories** or **give up your cookies and ice cream every night**, you make the decision. Either way will help you reach your weight loss goal.

DISC-based Coaching Session Questions

The Behavioral Sobriety™ Coaching Program is very different from other coaching programs because we focus on DISCflex. We believe that if you ask questions designed to resonate at the client's behavioral level, they will have more impact on the outcomes your client will see.

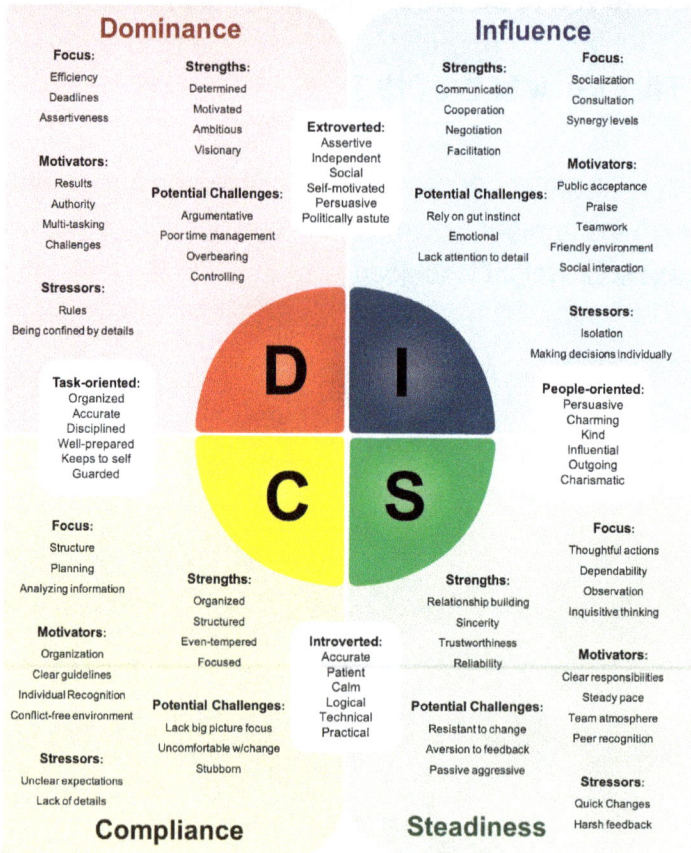

Dominance

Focus:
Efficiency
Deadlines
Assertiveness

Strengths:
Determined
Motivated
Ambitious
Visionary

Extroverted:
Assertive
Independent
Social
Self-motivated
Persuasive
Politically astute

Motivators:
Results
Authority
Multi-tasking
Challenges

Potential Challenges:
Argumentative
Poor time management
Overbearing
Controlling

Stressors:
Rules
Being confined by details

Task-oriented:
Organized
Accurate
Disciplined
Well-prepared
Keeps to self
Guarded

Influence

Strengths:
Communication
Cooperation
Negotiation
Facilitation

Focus:
Socialization
Consultation
Synergy levels

Motivators:
Public acceptance
Praise
Teamwork
Friendly environment
Social interaction

Potential Challenges:
Rely on gut instinct
Emotional
Lack attention to detail

Stressors:
Isolation
Making decisions individually

People-oriented:
Persuasive
Charming
Kind
Influential
Outgoing
Charismatic

Compliance

Focus:
Structure
Planning
Analyzing information

Motivators:
Organization
Clear guidelines
Individual Recognition
Conflict-free environment

Strengths:
Organized
Structured
Even-tempered
Focused

Introverted:
Accurate
Patient
Calm
Logical
Technical
Practical

Potential Challenges:
Lack big picture focus
Uncomfortable w/change
Stubborn

Stressors:
Unclear expectations
Lack of details

Steadiness

Strengths:
Relationship building
Sincerity
Trustworthiness
Reliability

Focus:
Thoughtful actions
Dependability
Observation
Inquisitive thinking

Motivators:
Clear responsibilities
Steady pace
Team atmosphere
Peer recognition

Potential Challenges:
Resistant to change
Aversion to feedback
Passive aggressive

Stressors:
Quick Changes
Harsh feedback

(Diagram center: **D** **I** / **C** **S**)

BACK TO THE BEGINNING

Now that you've learned what types of questions to ask, we are going back to the beginning, in a sense. This section contains suggestions of questions that are DISC Factor specific. You will notice these suggested questions tie into the client's 'Book About Me' workbook. We have provided targeted questions to ask for each section showing how to ask specific questions to match each of the DISC Factors. Ideally, you'll know your client's scores in each factor and tailor your coaching sessions to the client's unique behavioral pattern.

YOU CAN ASK THE SAME QUESTION IN FOUR DIFFERENT BEHAVIORAL WAYS

In this section, you'll look at how to effectively swap out the same question for the four DISC Factors. We believe it's best if a Recovery Coach poses questions in a behavioral style that will ring true to the client. If a client is more thoughtful and more prone to self-inflicting pain (Elevated Steadiness/Strategy Factor), the coach should pose their questions in a way that impacts elevated S verbiage. "George, in thinking through how you're going to communicate with Sarah about what you need to do for the next month, what are some of the things that are causing you internal pain?" The same question to an elevated Dominance Factor individual (quick paced, results-oriented, impulsive) might be posed like this: "George, let's look at the conversation you're soon to have with Sarah about what you need to do for the next month. We discussed putting your thoughts together before you talk to her. What are some of the things that you are going to focus on when you are explaining the results you expect to see?"

As you can see, the message posed differently might impact different clients at their behavioral core. When you go through this section, start looking at how the client's DISC Factors affect how you might pose the question. The more questions you examine, the more this concept will infiltrate your mind. When this occurs, your Self-Talk will change. You'll find that you will start tailoring your questions and verbiage to other people's behavioral patterns automatically. The more you focus on doing this, the better you'll become at this coaching skill.

Your job as a Behavioral Sobriety™ Coach is to ask questions that motivate the client to act in accordance with their recovery efforts. As you ask these types of DISC-based questions, you'll uncover some behavioral patterns that might help them get serious about how to own their boundaries and address their recovery efforts. One of the ways you can assess how motivated your client is in their recovery efforts is to monitor how they are doing in their 'Book About Me' workbook activities and readings.

We suggest that you open up a 'Consequences Discussion' about your expectations for their assignments. As part of this discussion, we suggest using DISC-based Q&A to underscore the importance of the 'Book About Me' workbook activities and the necessity of sticking to learning schedules.

CONSEQUENCES Q&A FOR COMPLETING OR NOT COMPLETING ACTIVITIES AND HOMEWORK:

1. Explain to the client that it is important they live up to their obligations and promises made in the coaching sessions.

2. Explain the potential consequences of non-adherence.

    a. Wasted time.

    b. Cause unnecessary stress.

    c. Feelings of disappointment, sense of failure, low self–esteem, low self–worth, feeling unaccomplished, self–loathing, apathy, guilt, or shame.

    d. Put these in terms of their DISC Pattern:

        -   **Dominance Factor:** *What were the results of procrastination or not completing assignments in the past? Did that behavior hurt or help?*

        -   **Influence Factor:** *What affect has procrastination or not completing assignments had on your relationships in the past? Did that behavior hurt or help?*

        -   **Steadiness/Strategy Factor:** *What embarrassing, or internally painful effect has procrastination or not completing assignments had in the past? Did that behavior hurt or help?*

        -   **Compliance Factor:** *Have you ever planned to do something but then you let procrastination or not completing assignments stop you from getting things done on time? Did that behavior hurt or help?*

3. Detail how each section in the workbook and every activity will address an area for their recovery efforts. Ideally you should do this in terms that will resonate with their recovery goals in DISC language.

Start Asking DISC-based Questions

TARGET HOW THE CLIENT STARTED DOWN THE PATH

Some addicts say that their substance of choice is the key that opened a locked door. Some people say that the minute they put the key in the lock, their life changed forever. For example, the first time they used cocaine, they thought: *"This is wonderful! I gotta get some more of that!"* and they were hooked. The key fit the lock. It's the same with some gamblers, sex or food addictions, or those who crave nicotine.

For others addiction seems to creep up, and before you know it, the slippery slope has you in a situation where you can't grab onto anything to get yourself out. We understand that society contributes in a big way. Take alcoholism: Whether you're ringing in the New Year, going to a concert, or watching your favorite team, the media glorifies events like these with corks and beer caps popping. Knowing this, there are certain behavioral tendencies that are linked to the four DISC factors.

Here is a reminder of what the DISC Factors are. Remember these as you look at the suggested DISC-based questions you can ask the client as they go through each activity in the 'Book About Me' workbook. Please use these as a guideline and come up with additional questions and follow up questions that work for you and your clients.

DOMINANCE	Your need for **control, how fast you like to get results,** and your source of **ambition.** Whenever you are feeling **self-motivated**, you are using your **'D' factor**.
INFLUENCE	Your need for **communication, interaction with others,** and your source of **persuasion**. Whenever you are feeling **talkative**, you are using your **'I' factor**.
STEADINESS	Your need for **preparation**, working things out, soul-searching, consideration and **thoughtfulness** as well as your need for comfort prior to taking action. When you are being **strategic** or **go out of your way to help someone**, you are using your **'S' factor.**
COMPLIANCE	Your need for **structure, adherence to rules,** and your source of **organization**. When you become **extremely focused on completing your tasks according to expectations**, you are using your 'C' factor.

Here are some examples of questions and their DISC-based counterparts to get your coaching sessions started:

WHERE DID YOUR ADDICTION BEGIN?

- **Dominance Factor:** *What were the results of your addiction?*
- **Influence Factor:** *How did your addiction affect your relationships?*
- **Steadiness/Strategy Factor:** *What were the major pain points of your addiction?*
- **Compliance Factor:** *What rules did you break and feel bad about during the later stages of addiction?*

HOW DID IT PROGRESS?

- **Dominance Factor:** *What degree of momentum/speed of decision making do you think occurs in your behavior when you decide to do something that isn't good for you? Do you think that sometimes stopping before acting might have changed some things for the better? For examples, what were some of the results of your quick pace on your addiction?*
- **Influence Factor:** *How did the friends change as your addiction progressed?*
- **Steadiness/Strategy Factor:** *As your addiction progressed, did you find yourself getting more moody, depressed, disappointed in yourself or something internally painful?*
- **Compliance Factor:** *Tell me about how you adjusted your schedule, habits and how your tried to square with your need for order as your addiction progressed.*

WHEN DID YOU REALIZE ADDICTION WAS A REAL ISSUE FOR YOU?

- **Dominance Factor:** When did you come to the realization that the results of your addiction weren't working for you anymore?
- **Influence Factor:** Did you ever feel insecure about your future and losing friends and becoming more and more isolated? Did the realization that your addiction wasn't working for you anymore happen because of a conversation with someone else or did you come to that conclusion alone?
- **Steadiness/Strategy Factor:** Did you ever feel depressed about your future or were you becoming more and more isolated from those you truly care about? How did the realization that your addiction wasn't working for you anymore happen?
- **Compliance Factor:** When you come to the realization that the results of your addiction weren't working for you anymore, did you immediately come up with some kind of plan to get you out and keep you on track with recovery efforts or are you looking for one now?

WHAT HAS WORKED FOR YOU SO FAR?

- **Dominance Factor:** What are the results of your recovery efforts so far? Are things happening quickly or slowly in your view?
- **Influence Factor:** What are the results of your recovery efforts so far? Do you feel better about talking them through now or are you still a bit raw and feel that you're not quite there yet?
- **Steadiness/Strategy Factor:** What are the results of your recovery efforts so far? Do you think you are a bit more able to figure out what makes you less anxious and more energized?

And do you want talk about some strategies to help you get more active? Do you think this discussion might help come up with some ways to deal with the depression you've been telling me about?

- **Compliance Factor:** What are the results of your recovery efforts so far? Do you think you are a bit more able to figure out some plans for this coming week to help you be less anxious and more energized? You mentioned you want to talk about a checklist to help you get more active. I wrote down that you want help coming up with some ways to deal with the depression you've been telling me about. Have you started putting together a list or a plan yet?

Habits Form Because of Addiction

For those who do abuse substances, these 'addiction norms' begin to spill over into all events and ultimately, into alone time, too. Habits emerge. In your coaching sessions, you'll undoubtedly spend some time talking about habits and how they formed. Perhaps it was a slow process, perhaps it was quick. A client goes from toasting annually when the ball drops in Times Square to toasting daily for life's normal events: A project completed, a section of dry wall installed, having a great meeting or making a sale, or surviving a tough day of parenting. Whew, that was a rough one! Sun setting? Calls for a beer or another glass of wine! If you examine all of these, there were lines that were crossed. Those can't be undone, but clients can certainly learn great lessons by examining them. Your questions can help them do that effectively in their own behavior style. Let's do an activity so you can practice.

ACTIVITY

Rewrite these questions for each of the DISC Factors:

What did those 'lines crossed' look like?

Dominance Factor: ______________________________

____

____

Influence Factor: ______________________________

____

____

Steadiness/Strategy Factor: ______________________

____

____

Compliance Factor: _____________________________

____

____

Did you know the line was being crossed when you were doing it? If so, what should you have done at those moments in time?

Dominance Factor: _____

_____

_____

Influence Factor: _____

_____

_____

Steadiness/Strategy Factor: _____

_____

_____

Compliance Factor: _____

_____

_____

Looking at those 'lines crossed', ask yourself: What can I do today (and moving forward) to make sure they don't get crossed again?

Dominance Factor: _____
_____
_____

Influence Factor: _____
_____
_____

Steadiness/Strategy Factor: _____
_____
_____

Compliance Factor: _____
_____
_____

Have the client look at this question: **What do my boundaries have to include, sound like, and be connected to for me to really 'own' them?**

Dominance Factor: _____

_____

_____

Influence Factor: _____

_____

_____

Steadiness/Strategy Factor: _____

_____

_____

Compliance Factor: _____

_____

_____

DISC-based Questions

Complementing Your Coaching Sessions with 'A Book About Me' DISC-based Questions

WHY THE WORKBOOK LESSONS ARE IMPORTANT

Any recovery program is only as good as the work the client puts in. We designed the **DISCflex Recovery: A Book About Me** workbook to help drive accountability.

- What happens when the coach is not around?
- Do the lessons stop?
- Is the client still working the program and motivated to learn and self-examine?
- Are they ahead or lagging according to progress expectations?

A Recovery Coach should recognize when clients put in the extra time and effort to work through their workbook their efforts. Keeping track of progress in the Client Sign Off sheet and checking off completed items/training in their workbook will help give clients a sense of accomplishment as well as providing a measuring stick for tangible work they have put in. Each time a client comes to a meeting and gets recognition/sign off for their efforts they will feel good and be more likely to want to continue delving deeper into the workbook.

Building this pattern of small achievements and recognition will build momentum towards more success.

"Success is the sum of small efforts - repeated day in and day out." – Robert Collier

Questions that pair to the 'Book About Me' workbook sections:

VALUES SECTION:

INITIAL QUESTION: WHAT DO YOU FEEL IT TAKES TO MAINTAIN SUCCESSFUL RECOVERY?

Questions if the client does not know what his or her values are:

What are some important things that were taught to you growing up?

D – How can you channel these to help your recovery efforts?
I – How can you tap into the warm feelings and important lessons you remember from childhood to help your recovery efforts?
S – How can you tap into the love your felt to capture the important lessons you remember from childhood to help your recovery efforts?

C – How can you reach back and remember the important lessons from childhood to help you better structure and make plans for your recovery efforts?

Think of someone you love. Why do you love that person? What is it you value about them?

D – How can you let them know you appreciate them and what they've done for you?

I – How can you let them know you appreciate their love and friendship?

S – How can you let them know you appreciate their loyalty and the deep connection you have?

C – How can you let them know you appreciate how they've helped shaped your life?

What would you like people to remember about you?

D – When you think about the results you want and the things you value in your life, at the end of the day how would you like people to remember you for your efforts and determination?

I – When you think about the friendships you want and the people you value in your life, at the end of the day how would you like people to remember you for your efforts and personality?

S – When you think about the connections and caring you have for others and the things you value in your life, at the end of the day how would you like people to remember you for your efforts and thoughtfulness?

C – When you think about the preparation and planning you've done, the progress you hope you'll make by working your plan, and the things you value in your life, at the end of the day how would you like people to remember you for your efforts and follow through?

> Often in life we forget the things we should remember, and remember the things we should forget.

WANTS VERSUS NEEDS ACTIVITY:

> People always want more. But sometimes we ruin what we already have by searching for what we don't need.

What does the word "need" mean to you?

D – When you think about things you need, how do you think they affect your recovery effort results, specifically talking about motivation, follow through, and determination in two ways:

a.   If you have them?
b.   If you can't get them yet?

I – When you think about things you need, how do you think they affect your recovery effort results, specifically talking about motivation, insecurity, friendships, and determination in two ways: 1. If you have them? 2. If you can't get them yet?

S – When you think about things you need, how do you think they affect your recovery effort results, specifically talking about motivation, strategy and changes they require (and you might not like making) in two ways: 1. If you have them? 2. If you can't get them yet?

C – When you think about things you need, how do you think they affect your recovery effort results, specifically talking about motivation, organization and planning in two ways: 1. If you have them? 2. If you can't get them yet?

Use similar verbiage for each of the four DISC Factors to adjust these questions to the client's behavior:

What does the word "want" mean to you?
How can you tell the difference between the two?
How does it feel when you get what you want?
How does it feel when you have all you need?

FEELINGS AND EXTERNAL SENSORY INPUT MOTIVATIONAL INTERVIEWING QUESTIONS

D – How can you direct/command your feelings to be positive?
I – How will your negative feelings affect others?
S – If you are going into a negative situation, what tools can you bring to help you stay positive?
C – What are some self–governed rules you can make to stay positive?

REPROGRAMMING MEMORIES

D – What would you like your memory to be like right now?

I – How would it sound if you told your positive memory to others?

S – What kind of energy would you like others to feel about your new memory?

C – How can you structure your new memory to be positive?

ESCALATION OF EMOTIONAL INVOLVEMENT

D – How can you prevent your negative emotions from manifesting into behaviors?

I – How would it affect you if others saw you negatively?

S – What steps can you take to prevent your loved ones from getting hurt by your negative emotions?

C – How can you organize your thoughts to stay on a positive track?

WHAT DOES MY CURRENT CHARACTER REFLECT?

D – **What** are some characteristics that prevail even when you don't want them to?

I – What have others stated they don't like about you?

S – What positive traits do you possess that can benefit yourself and others?

C – What negative traits do you carry that disrupt the process of your recovery

FEAR – WHERE DOES IT COME FROM?

D – Tell me about a time you made a snap decision that you instantly regretted.

I – Tell me about a time you made a decision that made you feel rejected by others.

S – Tell me about a time you made a decision without thinking that hurt others.

C – Tell me about a time you made a decision that made you feel uncomfortable and unorganized.

SYSTEMATIC DESENSITIZATION

D – What has been the result of a fear you have been unwilling to confront?

I – How could you use your "good fears" to help other people?

S – What does avoiding your fears say about your self–acceptance?

C – What do you think could happen if you maintained your courage?

OVERCOMING FEAR

D – What negative thoughts overcome your positive thoughts and how does that feed your "bad fear"? What could you instantly tell yourself to feed your "good fear"?

I – How could you influence your thoughts to feed your "good fears"?

S – What is a solid strategy/plan to assist you in overcoming your "bad fear"?

C – What rules could you set for yourself to help you accomplish overcoming your "bad fear(s)"?

DEALING WITH FEARS

D – What is a fear–based belief that hinders your progress in recovery?

I – How does your fear inhibit your social environment?

S – How does fear prevent your recovery strategy?

C – How has fear effected the standards you have set for yourself in the past?

TIPS TO KEEP A POSITIVE ATTITUDE

D – What is something you have said to yourself in the past that has had an immediate positive effect?

I – What is something positive you have said to someone in the past and how can you apply that to yourself?

S – What is a thoughtful statement you have told someone and how can you apply that to yourself?

C – What positive thoughts can you tell yow–self that will keep your recovery on track?

TIPS TO OVERCOME MY OBSESSION

D – **What** is a persistent thought that immediately stops your progress in recovery? What is something you could tell yourself to break that obsession?

I – What is an obsession that has a negative impact on your friendships?

S – How does obsessing interrupt your recovery plan?

C – What are some rules you can create to practice when you begin to obsess?

CHANGING NEGATIVE HABITS

D – What is something you want to see happen in the near future? (30 days)

I – How can having a healthy goal help those around you?

S – How can having positive habits add to your recovery strategy?

C – How can practicing positive habits help structure your desired outcome for recovery?

WHAT MOTIVATES ME?

D – What is a motivator, that you can use to help your recovery right now?

I – What is a motivator you can use to help those around you to support your recovery?

S – What is a motivator you can use to plan your recovery?

C – What is a motivator that falls into the rules you will establish regards to your recovery?

Talk: Then act.

Say it: Then show it.

Promise it: Then prove it.

Active Listening without Judgment

If we hope to get people to open in coaching sessions and allow us to see what really makes them tick, we need to engage in active listening. When we do, we create circumstances that encourage them to open up, engage more, and have a deeper level of communication with us.

Always try to remember that we were all born with two ears and one mouth. That is the same ratio that makes you a good communicator during coaching sessions: minimum of 2 parts listening; one part talking. Active listening involves the use of your highest level of auditory skills. Active listening can be very effective if you want to understand more about a person's values and beliefs, as well as what's truly important to them. It is also important to first listen before we can logically expect others to trust us.

ACTIVE LISTENING HAS SEVERAL COMPONENTS:

1. Context and content: Understanding the words spoken in the context they were intended. Pay attention to make sure you hear the actual words the client says. Have agreement of the framework, issue, opportunity, or the situation being discussed.

2. Clarification: Ensure that you clear up any potential misunderstanding of basic meanings.

3. Evaluation: Determine the present state versus desired state of the situation according to communication goals. What needs to be done with the information being communicated? Does something need 'fixing', or does the client simply need to vent? Are you expected to be a sounding board or are you expected to offer options and ask to follow up questions?

4. *Reaction/Response:* Provide verbal or body language messages that relay that you have a grasp of what the client is communicating. NEVER interrupt. Interrupting shows that you are disrespectful because you haven't listened until the end of the person's words. If you interrupt, you've already thought of your response before the person finished. None of these is appropriate for active listening.

Active listening involves giving the person who is speaking certain communication cues so that they get the impression that you're really listening to what they have to say, and that you care. Let's look at how this might work. Imagine that you were a client trying to get a point across and that you felt nervous.

HERE ARE TWO DIFFERENT SCENARIOS:

1. Suppose the person you're talking to is looking in a notebook the whole time, making notes, and never making eye contact with you. Occasionally, they might mutter "mm-hmm," but other than that, nothing indicates they are PRESENT in your conversation.

2. Now, imagine that the other person nods along with you, interjects at the right moments, and asks you relevant questions about the information you're giving. They tilt their head giving the impression that their ears are working. They also smile at the appropriate moments and never interrupt. Even better, they pause for a moment before they answer or respond to you. In this way, you realize that they've taken the time to listen thoughtfully to your comments and respond to your words appropriately.

Obviously, the second situation would make you feel more comfortable.

SIGNS OF ACTIVE LISTENING

As you can tell from what's already been said, active listening essentially amounts to putting across the 'signals' of active listening. When you communicate, the more you send the signal that you're actively listening, the more likely someone will be open with you.

Active listening involves the use of your highest level of auditory skills. It also involves giving the

person who is speaking certain communication cues so that they get the impression that you're really listening to what they have to say. When you communicate, the more you send the signal that you're actively listening, the more likely someone will open. Here are some signs of active listening:

- Eye contact and taking note of eye accessing cues.
- Nodding along with what a person is saying.
- Giving emotional cues to show that you're engaged such as laughing, smiling, and
- frowning. Your face and posture, your eyes and breathing all show that you're really engaging with what they're saying. You should take care to laugh when appropriate, or to smile or frown when the occasion calls for it. Just let yourself 'be in the moment'. Be 'fully present' and make yourself show that you are listening intently.

In responding, take on the appropriate emotional tone. If they are excited, you should be somewhat excited, too. Mirroring their emotions and feelings is a powerful way to connect. Of course, always remember to 'be appropriate' in your mirroring. What else can you mirror to show you're listening intently? If they are serious about the subject matter, you should be serious. Remember that body language and facial expressions are critically important in establishing trust and rapport. Creating and maintaining trust and rapport is critical during coaching sessions.

Active Listening
- Hearing Content
- Listening for Feeling
- Observing Body Language
- Neutral Technique
- Paraphrasing
- Self-Awareness
- Reflection
- Questioning
- Clarifying Technique
- Summarizing

VERBAL RESPONSIVENESS

You can respond verbally to show you are listening. When appropriate, you can interject with a statement that shows that you've been through what the person is talking about and that you understand it. Often, a simple statement of "I've been there before," or "I understand what you're saying" are enough to really get a person to open.

VERBAL BACKTRACKING, PARAPHRASING, AND SUMMARIZING

Other effective techniques for reading and understanding another person is to use verbal backtracking, paraphrasing, or summarizing:

VERBAL BACKTRACKING:

1. Verbal backtracking is used to can clear up any possible confusion or misunderstandings before they have arisen. You circle back to an earlier place in the conversation, asking for clarification, or asking questions during a conversation. It is basically just asking questions during a conversation to:
   a. Give the impression that you're listening intently, and
   b. Make sure that you truly understand what the other person is saying.

2. To use verbal backtracking effectively:
   a. Every so often repeat back what the client just said in the form of a question.
   b. Get your delivery spot-on: Try not to seem confused, but rather open-minded and curious, as if you're really trying your best to understand them.

c. You can say something like: "So if I understand you correctly, you're trying to put the point across that your peers need to be more effective in working together on group activities? I am hearing frustration. Is that accurate?"

3. In addition to aiding your understanding, verbal backtracking also has the benefits that it forces the person in question to actively question and/or clarify what they've said to you. Here's what happens:

   a. As you ask a person about what they've said, they must consciously call it to mind and ask themselves if they really meant it.

   b. They also are forced to explain their standpoint more clearly or to clarify their expectations a bit better. As you do this, you're naturally setting them up to engage in influential repartee with you.

PARAPHRASING:

Paraphrasing is a little different from backtracking. You restate a portion of the conversation with the explicit purpose of clarifying it or letting the person know that you understand their expectations. When you paraphrase you should try not to use all of the exact same words that the other person used. When you paraphrase, your words don't need to be posed in the form of a question. But again, they should always be your own words, not the client's. With paraphrasing you restate a portion of the conversation with the explicit purpose of clarifying it in terms that you would use. You do this to let the person know that you understand what they're saying from your experience and standpoint.

SUMMARIZING:

Summarizing is another tactic to show people that you were listening properly to them. When you summarize, you usually take large sections of the conversation and reduce them to their essentials. In summarizing you provide the gist of what your understanding is of what the person said. You should only summarize the key areas or the main points -- those that are worth noting or going over or those that need clarifying. When you summarize, you put the main ideas or points of the conversation into your own words. Remember, this summary is the general idea in a brief form where you focus on the heart of the matter.

MAKE SURE YOU AGREE ON EVERYONE'S UNDERSTANDING

When you paraphrase or summarize another person's words during conversation, make sure that you are looking for body language and vocal quality clues as to whether they agree with your summarization or paraphrasing. This is critically important. Active listening depends on feedback and a deep understanding of what the person is trying to say.

Let's step back for a moment. If you know that people want to be understood and accepted; how do you let them know that they are?

People feel valued and acknowledged when you show that you are willing to understand them. That means you must listen. However, effective listening is harder than it might seem. In fact, many people engage in ineffective listening. Let's look at what these might be.

Simply put, there are five major types of 'less than optimal' or ineffective listening behaviors that people tend to engage in. To help you identify if you might have fallen prey to these, let's take a critical look at each one of them in turn. Just as important, as you are going through this section, think of what you might do if you see your clients are ineffectively listening.

HERE ARE SOME INTERESTING QUESTIONS:

How might you bring this to their attention?

How do you think this information might help them in their relationships?

How do you think it might help/hurt their recovery efforts?

PRETEND LISTENING

The first type of ineffective listening is pretend listening. When you engage in pretend listening you give someone else the impression that you're listening to what they're saying when you're tuning them out. Oftentimes this isn't malicious. You just might have too much on your own mind to listen to what is being said. In pretend listening, you don't pay enough attention to the subject matter at hand.

How can the speaker pick up on pretend listening? When asked for a response, the listener typically brushes off the speaker without providing information or much thought about the issue. The goal of pretend listening is to look like you're listening, but to get out of conversation without much personal investment. Other times, pretend listening, or brushing people off, occurs deliberately. When you participate in this type of listening, you might look as if you are actively listening, but you really are not. Even though you might be making eye contact and giving off receptive body language, you are completely missing or ignoring what the person in saying.

> Most people do not listen with the intent to understand; they listen with the intent to reply.

Here's an example of pretend listening:

> *Person A says:* "I then told him that I was really going to have to put some thought into this issue before I gave him a firm answer. I just don't know what to do. Got any thoughts?"
> *Person B responds:* "Yes, I think that you always come up with the best solution. I don't think my input would be better than yours."

CONSEQUENCES AND SOLUTION TO PRETEND LISTENING

As you can see person "B" is not really listening to person A. Because of this, they do not fully understand each other. Person A really is looking for understanding and input from person B. By pretend listening, Person B is being disrespectful. Of course, this should be avoided! The first step to doing this is to be consciously aware of whether you're really paying attention to what the person is saying. To do this, turn off your self-talk and internal dialog so that the conversation between you and the other person is the only conversation filling your thoughts. The best way to accomplish this is to be *fully present and attentive*. Put all other thoughts out of your head except for what the person is saying at that moment. Imagine yourself in their shoes, and how important this might be to them. This will go a long way in getting rid of the negative ramifications of pretend listening.

SELECTIVE LISTENING

The next type of listening is selective listening. When you are participating in selective listening you are taking listening one step farther than with pretend listening. With selective listening, you are listening to what the person is saying but only hearing parts of what is being said -- the parts that interest you. Once again, this is might not be intentional. Sometimes it's an unconscious process or worse, a habit. Or it could simply be that your subconscious mind is filtering out only the parts of speech that you find most important for very good reasons. You might be trying to remember only the pertinent points to summarize what the speaker is saying.

THE FOLLOWING IS AN EXAMPLE: OF SELECTIVE LISTENING:

Person A says: "I told her I would go to a meeting with her three months ago, and she picks this day to ask me! But this is a once in a life time baseball game you're talking about here. I wonder what I should do."

Person B responds: "Speaking of baseball, did you see that horrible call the umpire made last night? The runner was definitely out."

CONSEQUENCES AND SOLUTION TO SELECTIVE LISTENING

Whatever the case, selective listening will not lead to a complete understanding of others, and as you can imagine from the last example, it can really tick someone off! Paying conscious attention to how you listen to people will be the best way to put a stop to this. Selective listening can lead you to misidentify the real topic of someone's communication. With selective listening you hear only what you want to hear. In this example, person B was probably thinking about last night's baseball game in their subconscious. The word 'baseball' triggered their subconscious thoughts and it became all they could focus on. As said, it takes real conscious effort to take listening a step farther and pay attention to the whole conversation -- the content and context of what the person is trying to say. To truly understand someone, you must listen to all that they are saying. As you can imagine, this is imperative during coaching sessions.

ADVISING TOO SOON

The next form of ineffective listening is called 'advising too soon'. 'Advising too soon' occurs when you give someone advice without them first seeking it. It also happens when someone tries to 'fix things' rather than allowing the client to explain ALL of the situation they are grappling with. Much like rapport, advising someone or even providing options to consider is something that you must earn. When you give someone advice too early, they might naturally be resistant to it. This will happen regardless of whether the advice or suggestions are valuable or not. Therefore, for the sake of communication, building relationships, and showing that you understand the other person and respect them, you should avoid giving advice or offering suggestions and options until the time is right. You must listen for the appropriate moment to provide suggestions and/or give advice. You also must decide if your advice is wanted or appropriate.

NOTE #1: Please remember, that as a Behavioral Sobriety™ Coach, we cannot stress enough that you should not direct the client. You should always provide multiple options and talk through the pros and cons. The same is true when asked for what to do or suggestions.

NOTE #2: Sometimes, advice is exactly what isn't needed. Sometimes simply letting the person talk things through will help THEM come up with their own answer, so that you never have to provide any options, much less advice!

Back to 'advising too soon'. Minimally, you must listen for when they solicit advice or information from you before you leap in to 'advising too soon'. Advice should only be given when you truly understand the other person and when rapport has been established.

Look at this example:

Kim meets up with her coworker, Sarah, and is introduced to Sarah's boyfriend, Matthew. Kim and Sarah are having a conversation when Kim says "I never feel like going out any more. All I normally do is go home straight after a meeting. I don't go early or stick around afterwards." Before Sarah has a chance to respond, Matthew gives Kim some advice, "You've got to get out and interact. Recovery is best done with others. If you don't interact, you won't have the supporter network you need to support long-term recovery. And that's not cool!"

CONSEQUENCES AND SOLUTION TO ADVISING TOO SOON

This is an example of when someone offers advice when the timing is not appropriate, and the trust isn't high enough. Matthew does not yet understand Kim or her situation. How could he? He's only just been introduced to her. He has not yet gained trust and rapport with her. At the very least, it's presumptuous of him to offer advice without understanding. It's easy to see that Kim isn't going to be very receptive to the advice, however on point or valuable. Kim would be more likely to take the advice if it came from someone who fully understood her and at least picked up on the context and intentions of what she was saying at that moment.

JUDGING

Another type of ineffective listening is judging. Judging occurs when you immediately make a decision without first actually listening to what they have to say. Judgment is most often based on a bias. Perhaps you are swayed in a direction by your personal values and beliefs, and when a subject comes up, these are what guides your judgment. When this happens, you immediately shut down open-minded communication and along with it any possibility of understanding precisely how the other person thinks.

For instance, take this example:

Person A says: "I'm starting to think that I just don't fit in with old friends I used to hang out with anymore. I find myself avoiding them more and more. I'm not returning their texts or calls."

Person B responds: "You just need to lighten up. You don't have to avoid them completely. You can control it even if you're tempted by what they're doing. You just don't like the fact that you have changed, and they haven't. You need to try to help them, too."

Not only does this count as advising, but person B also made a negative judgment about the first person saying they are not helpful. This destroys rapport instantly. To avoid this type of listening, don't just jump to conclusions. Take time to find out why the person you're communicating with feels the way they do or why they made the comment they did. Take the time to discover what will help build trust and rapport. The person you are communicating with will be more accepting of your 'judgments' and/or preconceptions when you give them at the appropriate time.

PROBING

Probing is a method of questioning designed to make the person provide information they might not want to give out. Probing often makes people uncomfortable and wary. When a person probes, they ask a targeted question, and then listen for the response. If the response isn't 'enough', the person probes again, until they are satisfied they have the information they need. In coaching sessions, you sometimes must probe. Clients rarely answer all the questions that need to be addressed without probing, prompting, or the like. That's the nature of the beast.

So how do you probe and keep the relationship strong? The first thing to do is tell the person what you are doing. This is called 'fair warning'. Whenever you are going to do something you know might break rapport, tell the person. Here's an example: "John, I know that we've been dancing around your recovery efforts and activities last week. I'm going to ask you some pointed questions to figure out what's happening, and I'm going to keep probing for the facts until we get to something close to reality."

The secret of effective probing is a 'Catch 22'. Probing will not work unless rapport is established first and the person is open and willing to provide answers to your questions. The only reason they'll do this is when they feel that you are not going to use the information against them. So, knowing this, you should tell them why this information must come to the surface. "John, if we know what happened last week, we can get through it. If I don't know what's happening, how can we discuss some solutions?" "or "John, you know that full transparency, no secrets, discussing things that are uncomfortable,

is all part of knowing yourself best. So, let's just get it out on the table. The information will stay right here in this room. I promise. I can't help you help yourself if it doesn't come out."

If the person doesn't trust you or isn't responsive, they won't answer your questions no matter how deep or 'hard' you probe. It will be an awkward process that will get you nowhere. And if they do provide the information, they'll resent it. That's not great for coaching sessions at all! But on the flip side, if you have established a high level of trust and rapport with the client, probing isn't really needed. They should trust you enough to answer your questions without you 'digging' for the answer; the simple act of asking the right type of questions - not 'probing' - starts a conversation. How do you know the difference (if you feel like you are)? Additionally, if you only ask closed-ended questions when probing, your results will be less than desirable. If the questions are like 'pulling teeth' during a coaching session, you're probably probing.

Here is an example of probing that doesn't go well for the person trying to probe:

A: "How did your conversation with your sister go last week, Mary?"
B: "Okay, I guess."
A: "Learn anything about why she's been avoiding you?"
B: "Not really."
A: "Are you planning to call her again this week?"
B: "Haven't particularly thought about it yet."
A: "Why not?"
B: "I just haven't."

As you can see, probing did not get person A detailed answers to any of the questions that they asked person B. Person B clearly didn't want to be engaged. If probing continues, both participants are likely to become frustrated with each other. If you are the person probing, and you are not getting the appropriate responses from the person you're talking to, you should stop probing. It's as simple as that. If you don't stop, probing can make the situation worse.

However, there are times when probing is appropriate. When rapport is high, probing is an excellent way to procure information and keep the conversation ball rolling. Let's look at an example of what this would be like:

A: "How did your conversation with your sister go last week, Mary?"

B: "It was really great. My anxiousness was all for nothing! We talked for 45 minutes. Mostly about life. You know, like how we got to this point and how we miss each other."

A: "Learn anything that you particularly liked?"

B: "Well, I knew that grandpa was an addict. And I knew that he took part in an invasion in Normandy. It suddenly dawned on me that he was probably in the D-Day invasion. My sister asked how old he was, and we figured out he would have been about 24 years old. We both wondered if that's one of the reasons he drank so much. Because he went through a lot in the war and all. So, we're going to call my grandma and ask her if she thinks he'll be open to talking about his life. He's been sober about 30 years. We figured out that's also about the same age I realized I must change, too. I would love to ask him some questions! And my sister and I are doing it together. Plus, she said we can actually go visit him! I promised my sister that I would go with her. I'm excited!"

As you can see, there's a vast difference between employing probing when the other person is receptive and when they are not. When using this tactic, make the choice when to use it based on the response that you get in the person's willingness to be open. Active listening can be very effective if you want to understand more about a person's values and beliefs. It is important to first listen before you can effectively ask someone to trust you.

Too often we underestimate the power of touch or a hug. We discount the power of a listening, a smile, a heart-felt compliment, or the tiniest act of compassion and caring. Think of these like ripples in a person's life. At the right moment a small ripple can build, turning into a powerful tsunami that will change them forever. Your job as a coach: Create positive ripples.

Do's and Don'ts for Active Listening

DO:

DO ASK: If you are unsure, ask questions: If you're not sure what the person means, ask them questions like: "Do you mean this?" "Am I correct in my thinking that you meant...?" Never guess when you can simply ask the person directly. Hoping you guessed right does work for effective coaching sessions. Clarify. Clear up misunderstandings. Avoid confusion.

DO Overlook speech problems or when they don't choose the exact word you think they should: Please ignore anything that isn't perfect in a client's speaking or communication. Such things as **twitches,** tapping, an unusual voice, a high-pitched or squeaky voice, or a heavy accent are inappropriate to comment on. This is the same advice for any ill-chosen words the client might pick. Please remember that communication isn't perfect and cut people a lot of slack in this area. When people are in a coaching session, they aren't necessarily concentrating on their words especially when emotions run high or when they are thinking about their past and how to best move forward. Confusion inside the client's head sometimes exhibits itself in strange and wonderful ways. Listen, and don't nitpick petty inconsequential things while you are listening. Never let those things distract you from what's truly important during the coaching sessions. Just focus, focus, focus on listening! When you notice something different it may make it difficult to concentrate, but you must focus and do exactly that. You should concentrate on what is being said always.

DO Be open minded: Always be willing to consider new ideas and suggestions, especially when they come from the client. Just because you're a coach doesn't mean you know best or have all the answers! If you don't listen, you never learn anything new. Never assume you know exactly what the client should do. There are many paths to Behavioral Sobriety™. There are many options in recovery. Open-minded approach is an impartial and unprejudiced style. Showing that you are **receptive to new ideas or arguments** or that you're neutral, nonjudgmental, and nondiscriminatory is powerful.

DO Give a reaction: Make eye contact, nod if you agree, and interject phrase like "I'm happy to hear that", "How interesting!", "I can see that", or "I understand what you mean", assuming they don't interrupt the person's words. Provide confirmation: "Yes, I agree" or "No, you were right not doing that."

DON'T:

Don't assume or jump to conclusions: Human nature has people thinking a step or two ahead. But forming conclusions too soon, without adequate time to listen and evaluate is a sure-fire way of being wrong in many instances. Even worse, pre-thinking what you think the client is about to say next shuts down discussions and can really make a client frustrated or angry. Many misunderstandings and trust breakdowns occur because of this. Doing this is dismissive and rude!

Don't interrupt or self-talk/listen: Be present. Pay attention and take note of what is being said Confuse and HOW it is communicated. This takes concentration. If you are thinking ahead, talking to yourself inside your head, or thinking about your response, you aren't in active listening mode!

Don't judge: Judgment and bias are coaching session killers! Examine your personal biases (you all have them) and figure out a way to curtail them during coaching sessions.

Each person holds so much power within themselves that needs to be let out. Sometimes they just need a little nudge, a little direction, a little support, a little coaching, and the greatest things can happen.

- Pete Carroll

Provide Feedback to Provoke Thoughtful Responses

Preparing to Provide Feedback During a Coaching Session

WHY GIVE FEEDBACK?

Feedback coaching sessions are not an isolated, nor a one-sided event. Ongoing feedback is of critical importance. So is ongoing praise! But, often more important than the giving of feedback are the conversations and responses that happen because you've delivered it, and then praised your client for what they did with that feedback. When your clients respond to you about the feedback you've given them, you must take in what they say, process in effectively and reply, addressing all their concerns, perhaps dealing with negative emotions. You must anticipate some of the things they'll say or do and sort through their responses to get to a place where they understand why you gave the feedback. Next, the client should realize that feedback is given with a view to them taking corrective actions. The dialog should occur with a view to making plans to come up with suitable ways to resolve the feedback issue. Likewise, make certain they understand you'll keep your finger on the pulse of this issue, making certain you circle back to it until new behavior and/or habits are in place. Reiterate the reason for feedback: To make sure recovery efforts stay on track. This view should fuel momentum and make feedback a bit easier 'to swallow'.

LESS EXPERIENCE, MORE FEEDBACK

The primary goal of Recovery Coaching is to engage clients towards Behavioral Sobriety™. Clients ideally will take on accountability for their responsibilities and make improvements in their habits. But that's in an ideal world. This is recovery and that puts a different spin on things sometimes. This means that you'll probably be spending more time initially on less experienced clients to ramp up their skills and knowledge around recovery accountability. While at first it might seem counter-intuitive that you have less to talk about recovery accountability with your 'star clients' or those whom you've been coaching a while, think about this: By the time you've been coaching them for a while, they should have the 'recovery accountability thing' down pat.

Feedback and corrections take less time because you've already established what the process is. Clients already fully understand by giving feedback you're doing your best to shine light to help their recovery efforts. Therefore, as a Recovery Coach, you don't have to spend as much time 'explaining the process' or 'dealing with feedback feelings'. As clients initially engage with you and start to receive feedback from a Recovery Coach, it's sometimes tough to sort everything through emotionally. Nowhere is this tougher than receiving critical feedback. This is especially true if they're already feeling 'down on themselves' or a bit hopeless. Add this to the fact that most people aren't trained in how to RECEIVE FEEDBACK and you'll begin to get a sense of why spending lots of time upfront is important.

Logically then, inexperienced clients require more time to deliver and talk through your feedback. However, this doesn't mean that you stop providing consistent and timely feedback to ALL clients. You must do this on an ongoing basis, whenever warranted, if your clients are to have any hopes of improving their behavior and staying on track with recovery efforts. At the same time, you must be certain not to alienate those star players we mentioned. Always recognize their efforts and let them know why it is that you spend less time on their feedback as your coaching sessions progress. Explain that you realize they are on board and on track – because you know that they can take care of themselves better and better as your coaching sessions and their learning improves. This is a natural byproduct as your Recovery Coaching and time together continues.

PLAN AHEAD

You should always prepare for Providing Feedback or Delivering Evaluation Documentation During a Coaching Session ahead of time. There are many tactics that we'll discuss that you can use to give yourself the edge when facing a potentially tense coaching session. Each one of these should be exploited to make the best of the situation. Going into an evaluation blind, without facts and data to back you up, is never a good idea. You'll just be setting yourself up to get blindsided. The client could have an emotional outburst or become defensive. Therefore, with due preparation, most of this can be avoided.

SET THE TONE FOR THE SESSION

An evaluation should set the tone for the coming 'accountability period', establishing what goals and deliverables are important to recovery efforts now, having discussions and perhaps offering suggestions for how to best work towards those goals. What is an 'accountability period'? It's the agreed timeframe for deliverables and measurements. Ultimately, upcoming 'accountability periods' should provide clients with a frame of reference by which they can work more productively and effectively, improving themselves and advancing their goals (short and long term).

DO NOT DISCUSS...

There are certain **critical matters that you must never discuss or criticize** during a feedback coaching session (or at any other time for that matter). This might include subjects such as race, age, religion, politics, and sexual orientation. In general, avoid the kind of topics that might lead to allegations of discrimination or might get you into legal hot water.

NO IMPROVISATION!

Never, under any circumstances, improvise during a performance evaluation. Never "wing it". In a very literal way, lives might hang in the balance because of the feedback you provide. Feedback can help turn someone around, especially if it is delivered well. So, you should always approach the matter with that sense of importance and gravity. **By preparing thoroughly ahead of time, you can make certain that no matter what happens, you get your points across and the client leaves the coaching session knowing what it is that is expected of them performance-wise in the future.** By "winging it", you risk failing to properly communicate your ideas, or worse, running into conflicts that you're unprepared to dissolve or avoid. Possibly much more important, you will botch your dialogue and suggestions for improvement. Additionally, you might forget to set appropriate goals and metrics for the upcoming 'accountability period'.

HAVE A CLEAR AGENDA

Just like conducting regular coaching sessions, when you perform a client feedback session, you should have a clear agenda. Prepare a list of points that you want to go over during the session, and define an order to hit them in. Having an agenda laid out beforehand will help you to remember critical points if you get sidetracked by other discussions that come up. In general, the more organization and preplanning you can bring to the feedback process, the better it's likely to go.

USE MEASURABLE CRITERIA

The criteria that you use to constructively criticize or praise a client's recovery efforts and results should always be objective, which means that these should always be measurable. Don't just say that a client did "pretty good" or "rather badly". Instead, provide facts and figures that show what was expected of the client, compared to how the client behaved and performed. With hard numbers on the record, it's hard to disagree with a Recovery Coach's feedback. For example, a client might have had the goal of exercising more in the evenings. By looking at their sensor tracking stat, when the numbers were examined, it's not happening. As you can imagine, the client might want to argue that biking to work in the morning or climbing stairs should more than compensate for not meeting their evening activity goal. However, you must address this in the coaching sessions as part of their promises they didn't deliver. Think of this: What if everyone could argue which metrics should count and which shouldn't, after their agreements were made? What message are you sending as the Recovery Coach, to allow this to go unchecked? How would recovery efforts progress if clients weren't held accountable for all the goals they agreed to were part of their responsibilities? If this were allowed, why bother with goals, measures, objectives or recovery accountability at all?

BE OBJECTIVE

As we've mentioned before, being objective is one of the most critical aspects of conducting a feedback coaching session. During a feedback meeting, you must stick to the facts and rely on evidence when proving instances to back up your observations. **Discuss specific incidents** rather than relying on fallible sources like memory and hearsay. For example, you should say to the client, "You were absent from work on October 10, 11, and 12 with no formal notice. Your recovery success requires your attendance at work each day. You know that the only exception is to provide work and your Recovery Coach with a note from a doctor." Rather than saying, "You have missed more work days than you should." The first statement is clearly objective and leaves no room for debate because it uses hard facts and data. The more objective you are, the more specific you are with the facts, the less opportunities there are for the client to argue, debate the information, or get into unproductive conflict.

In general, the question of who is meeting expectations, who is exceeding them, and who is lagging is steeped in subjectivity. You can't be the Recovery Coach who is like other people. Your responsibility is to be objective and have the facts for any feedback your deliver. What makes feedback sessions go 'wrong'? Less than adequate communication of expectations and not enough feedback compound how badly feedback coaching sessions go. Not being objective and/or being ill-prepared can lead to quite a few emotional encounters with clients. In addition, clients who feel they were doing well do not take kindly to getting surprise feedback or when a Recovery Coach says something vague like he or she "feels" that the client 'could do better'. Be specific. Remove opinion and subjectivity from feedback coaching sessions as much as possible.

By using measurable data, observation, and information gleaned from other sources, you can deliver feedback, results, and behavior in an objective and predictable matter. If they listen to the feedback you consistently provide them, clients will have a good sense of their own recovery efforts versus expectations. They can do a 'gap analysis' at any given time to move forward with the recovery goals, locking in good decision making and acquiring better habits. Feedback can give a client very specific information about what is expected of them, and who (THE CLIENT) is accountable for failure or not reaching desired recovery results.

Prepare like you've never won.
Perform like you've never lost.

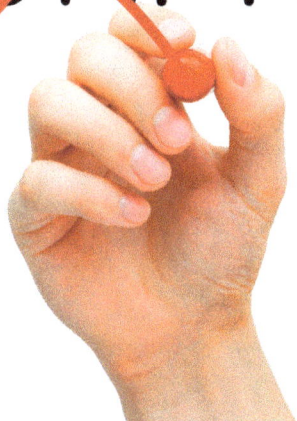

RESUME

Points for Your Feedback Coaching Sessions

Preparation for the Feedback Coaching session

MAP A COMMUNICATION PLAN AND REHEARSE YOUR DELIVERY

It pays to mentally rehearse for any feedback sessions. Mapping out a feedback communication plan means that you go over the topics that you plan to cover with the client. Based on your knowledge of them, you can anticipate the things that they're likely to say in return. You can anticipate your own reactions to their reactions. By doing this, you help yourself not to be taken off guard by unexpected turns in the flow of conversation. Be careful, however, not to get locked into so rigid a conversation structure that you end up totally unprepared to follow along with how the conversation goes! The flow of feedback sessions is important to recovery success. As a Recovery Coach, you must listen and allow the client to discuss their agenda points too. Remember, we advise the clients to do the same as their Recovery Coach. Come prepared and have agenda points to discuss.

Rehearse 'inside your head first'. Make any adjustments to the feedback you're going to provide. Next, say what you plan to say out loud. This works even if you are the only person who will hear it. A lot of feedback comes across by way of your gestures and tonality. You can get a sense of how it's going to sound and look to the client if you practice in front of a mirror. Sometimes by doing this, you can not only develop a more confident delivery, but also catch things that may be ambiguous, confusing or will take the discussion down a 'rat hole'. You also might pick up words or sentences that may sound subjective rather than fact and/or data based. Additionally, view your words through the client's lens. Have you listened to hear what the client might think of as frustrating or insulting? Have you tested your phrases to listen to what might make the client unnecessarily angry, combative, or defensive? Your delivery is important because it often forewarns how well (or badly) the client might take in your feedback. Your rehearsal allows you to change things so that the coaching session goes as well as it possibly can.

Focus on the client's behavior, never their character.

Discuss the Actions and BEHAVIOR; Never Criticize the Person's Character. When providing your findings and feedback, be certain to always phrase statements to the client in a fashion that makes it clear that it's the deliverables, actions, and behaviors you are specifically discussing, not the person's character or personal core values. Clients might still react negatively, but it's much more likely they'll take kindlier to "For the past two coaching sessions, you haven't completed the activities we agreed were important for you." This behavior makes it difficult to keep sessions productive. Plus, you must focus on doing things on time. Working on procrastination is one of this month's goals." rather than "Why can't you ever do what I ask on time?!"

MAINTAIN NEUTRALITY

It's important to maintain a sense of neutrality while providing feedback. The bottom line is that your life as a Recovery Coach won't change if your client doesn't live up to their responsibilities. This is their recovery efforts, not yours. If you must go over someone else's observations or negative comments from another supporter, and give your client some tough feedback, you might be tempted to say something like, "They sure can be hard sometimes, can't they?" to make the news go over easier. Resist this temptation. You cannot take sides on this. "Putting down' the observer lessens the impact of their observation. It is what it is. It's their reality and it needs to be brought out. Relationships are at stake. As a Recovery Coach, you must remain as neutral as possible in all matters such as this, so that if emotions rise or conflict begins, you're in the best position to defuse it.

BE CLEAR

When preparing your feedback, be sure that you plan your statements concisely. It's best to avoid artistry or wordiness altogether. Just speak as bluntly and plainly as you possibly can. Do so with Nobel Intent and a good heart. Use common words. Be direct and forthright. Being vague for the sake of sparing feelings will just lead to your ideas being misrepresented and misunderstood. Using clear, easy to understand words and keeping your sentences short and to the point will help the client to digest and remember them more easily.

THE MEETING PLACE MUST BE PRIVATE

All feedback and coaching discussions should be private. There is only one exception - when giving feedback during a dangerous situation where you need to bring in other parties such as a supporter/ representative to ensure order and safety. For this session, we will assume this is not the case. Never conduct a feedback coaching session in a public place. The potential for it going awry is simply too great. On one hand, the client might feel uncomfortable responding to what you say openly if there are other people around. On the other hand, if you provide feedback, they'll likely resent you for it if others are around to overhear. Before you conduct a feedback coaching session, make sure that you have a totally private and secure meeting place, where both parties feel comfortable. As a bonus, conducting a feedback discussion in private will make it seem more formal and thus more meaningful and memorable to the client.

AVOID CONFLICTS

Avoid conflicts when conducting a feedback coaching session by sticking to the facts and remaining neutral and objective. If you sense that the client is trying to take the discussion in an argumentative or unproductive direction, do what you must to reign them in. Once conflict begins, it's harder to defuse than if you cut it off before it ever has a chance to escalate. Study anger management and 'becoming defensive' to pinpoint the root causes of client frustration, anger, and/or 'desire to battle'.

BE COMPOSED AND CALM. NEVER LOSE YOUR COOL

The worst thing that a Recovery Coach can do during a feedback coaching session is to lose his/her cool and get into a heated discussion or an argument with the client. If this happens, the client will know this is an acceptable behavior during the coaching sessions. Plus, they'll potentially lose respect for you, try to goad you into doing it again in a future session, or not take your words as seriously as your actions. Instead they will be more likely to rebel against the process just for emotional gratification.

As such, if you're not confident that you can keep your cool during a feedback coaching session, use one of these tactics to keep a cool head. Reschedule the coaching session. Have someone else be present with you when you deliver this feedback. Rehearse with someone and get your delivery perfect. Stick rigidly to your agenda and insist that all counters or objectives be addressed at a later coaching session and or in writing. Pick a time when the client will be most receptive, and you will be most calm. Ideally, of course, you should be able to remain calm no matter who you're providing feedback to, but in extenuating circumstances where you have repeatedly delivered feedback to problematic clients with less than stellar responses, keep these options (and others like them) in mind.

Points for Delivering Feedback During a Coaching Session

ESTABLISH THE GROUND RULES

Before you carry out a feedback discussion, always set forth ground rules for how the conversation will proceed. These can be simple things like 'no personal attacks' or rules for moving through the 'housekeeping' issues, responses, follow up, paperwork or the agenda. It can include communication guidelines such as who should speak and when (no interrupting). No matter what the guidelines are, make sure that they help rather than hinder communication. Also, check that everyone involved is aware of them up front.

HERE ARE SOME SUGGESTIONS FOR GROUND RULES DURING THE FEEDBACK COACHING SESSION:

1. Confidentiality first. What is said in the coaching session, stays in the session unless parties agree to discuss with others. If anyone thinks harm to self or others will occur, they have a responsibility to share with predesignated appropriate parties.
2. Be fully present. Silence all cell phones, pagers, and sideline other distractions.
3. This is a 'haven' where it is expected that people will always be honest.
4. Be respectful and sensitive to others.
5. Refrain from using offensive language.

6. Listen to each other. Give everyone an opportunity to speak without interrupting.
7. Share feelings and experiences openly. Discuss options but never give advice.
8. Have a positive attitude. Accept the feedback without making judgments. Be thoughtful in any responses.

STATE THE PURPOSE OF YOUR FEEDBACK AND HOW IT MIGHT BE USEFUL TO THE CLIENT.

THE PURPOSE OF A FEEDBACK DISCUSSION IS TO GO OVER ANY DELIVERABLES OR PROMISES MADE SINCE THE LAST ACCOUNTABILITY PERIOD.

The goal is to discuss 'results versus expectations' with a view to moving forward with any changes or corrective actions. Tell the client what you'd like to cover is important. This opening statement gives the other person a heads-up about how the conversation will go. If the other person has requested feedback, a focusing statement will make sure that you direct your feedback toward what the person needs. Remember: Be clear and straight-to-the-point. Start with a strong statement: "In reviewing what you said, I have noticed that..." "I went through my notes about what activities were due, and I have a concern about...." "Recovery efforts require discipline. I want to give you some of my observations..." "I have put together some talking points from our last conversation..."

REITERATE THAT FEEDBACK IS SIMPLY PART OF THE PROCESS AND THAT IT CAN BE USEFUL.

A great Recovery Coach helps a client overcome any shortcomings and realize their true potential. But does the client know that? Some clients may view every feedback discussion as something like a 'disciplinary action' and be defensive from the start. In such cases, you can help them to relax and ensure a better feedback session if you're clear about what the point of the feedback is from the very beginning. Plus, it always helps to go over this just to make sure that everyone is on the same page. Start off the meeting by saying, "Thank you for meeting with me today. The purpose of this segment of our coaching session is to ensure your recovery efforts continue toward success outcomes, and help you reach your recovery goals. One of my responsibilities is to continuously provide you with feedback to make you aware of how your actions and behaviors might impact your recovery efforts. My goal in giving you feedback is specifically to help you see things you might not otherwise see. Hearing feedback is tough, but I hope you know that feedback, however painful, can be a great gift if taken well and with a view for improvement."

DESCRIBE SPECIFICALLY WHAT YOU HAVE OBSERVED - ONLY DISCUSS FACTS, DATA AND VERIFIABLE INFORMATION.

1.   **Make a list of the specifics of a bounded event or situation.** You never want feedback to be broad in nature. The more specific you are, the better. Plus, you don't want the client to go off on tangents because you've opened the door and/ or 'muddied the waters'. The thing you want to avoid is that the client will be able to diffuse the feedback by talking about something unrelated or insignificant. Compile your thoughts in a logical format. Include details that will substantiate the feedback you are giving. Example: Dates, times, people involved, promises made, and results can be important details. In addition, make sure that the specific situation you are there to discuss has enough detail to make it valuable feedback. In addition, whenever possible, remain objective and stick to what you have observed.

2.   **Be impartial.** When conducting a feedback coaching session, always be as impartial as possible. There may well be times when you must provide feedback to clients you really like, know that they've tried their best and you feel bad that you must tell them something that might make them unhappy, demotivated, or angry, or with whom you have had feedback problems in the past. It's ok that you might not 'like' your clients actions or current behavior. But you must be impartial and objective. You can never let your personal feelings, preferences, biases, or the like, enter the feedback coaching session. If you have trouble with this with some clients, take a cold hard look at why this might be happening. Try a different tactic. Have others

look at your evaluation if possible to make certain that you're being objective. You cannot let your personal feelings influence your Recovery Coaching Sessions or decisions.

3. **If you are providing third-party info, state that and allow that this information may be biased or blatantly untrue.** You must tell the client that you are open and listening to their view of the incident. You also must make them aware that you are not passing judgment of any kind, and that you are specifically providing feedback to discuss behavior and/or corrective actions for the future. Please note that you should only discuss the specific feedback that you have said you were going to in your opening statement. If you need to provide feedback on more than one thing, state this at the beginning of the meeting and discuss the order and process for segmenting these different feedback points. As much as possible, speak in absolutes and not generalities. An absolute uses words, like 'always' and 'never' versus 'sometimes' and 'not often'. If you use specific words, feedback coaching sessions tend to go better. "On Wednesday, when we chatted, I heard you raise your voice twice to people in the background when we were interrupted." For example: "Yesterday afternoon, when you were speaking with customers, I noticed that you kept raising your voice."

4. **Be Consistent and stick to your agenda.** Go over all the points that you intend to make and be certain that none of them contradict with one another. Also, if you make one statement, continue without detracting from it. If you make one proclamation about what is expected of the client but then retract it without

evidence to the contrary, they'll never know which feedback to take seriously and which is "okay" to ignore. Consistency is also important when conducting feedback coaching sessions in general. You must treat all clients fairly and equitably.

5. **Ask the client to think about the situation and let them know you want to get their view of the situation.**

6. **Give the other person an opportunity to respond without judging.**

7. **Make sure your words are heard and understood.** Consider this rule literally. Make sure that your "words" are heard. Oftentimes, the content, context or intent of your actual words will get obscured by other matters like an unintentional tone of voice, or the mood or state of mind that the client happens to be in. If they seem to be reacting inappropriately to something that you said during an evaluation, stop and confirm that they understood the content or context of your message. You must check that they're not reading into things that you didn't intend.

8. **Listen! A feedback coaching session is best with a robust dialog.** This means that you must remember to listen openly to what the client has to say. If the client is unwilling to respond or is tentative be ready with an opened-ended question. Keep quiet and look at the client which is a signal that you are waiting for a response. "Tell me, Jane, what are your thoughts on this?" "What's your view/position of this event/situation?" "What's going inside your head right now, thinking about this?" "What is your reaction to this?"

9. **Describe the possible consequences and other people's reactions.**

10. **Ask about what the client might think would happen if the behavior were to continue.** Explain the consequences of the behavior from a Recovery Coach's perspective, specifically as it relates to recovery efforts. If you can, depersonalize the event by providing examples of others that might have exhibited similar behavior and describe what happened to them and those they care about. By looking at what happened to others, the client can look more objectively at the behavior that is not desirable. Hopefully they can then figure out a way 'the other person' could have dealt with it better and relate that to themselves.

11. **After this discussion, steer back to the client's specific event and behaviors.** Discuss the desirable behavior and ways to avoid repeating the decision making or mistakes of the past. Ask them who in their circle might be affected by continued behavior and ask them to figure out the specific impact to that person. Having the client work through the potential reactions or consequences allows them to understand the impact their actions have on others. Example: "You told me that your girlfriend appeared angry, frustrated and embarrassed when she found out that you had not attended any meetings in the past week. You just told me that she was furious that you lied to her, saying that you went when you didn't. What are the consequences for that with trust in your relationship? What do you think you can do in the future to not lie to her and to deliver on your promises to her and yourself?"

ASK THE CLIENT TO THINK THROUGH SOME OPTIONS.

1. **Link Feedback and Suggestions to a Solution.** It does very little good just to provide feedback and then not have an improvement and follow up plan. While matters of not meeting recovery expectations on following through with recovery accountability deliverables need to be directly addressed, it's always critical to link any feedback you provide to the client to future outcomes and expectations. This means the coaching sessions must provide suggestions for improvement and a plan to move forward without the same behaviors repeating themselves. This 'feedback then plan to move forward' thinking will help the client to feel as if they're truly being assessed with their best recovery interests in mind.

2. **Consequences and Benefits: As the client goes through their options, have them talk through the consequences and benefits of each.** You are looking for specific suggestions from the client to move forward with this event/situation from this feedback coaching session.

3. **Options: Whenever possible only offer other options as a last resort if the client has exhausted all their thoughts and they still haven't come up with feasible solutions.**

4. **Understand limitations in coming up with solutions.** One exception to this is if the client isn't thinking through the options that might make sense to others who might be in a similar situation. **Not all clients have the answers for every situation they find themselves facing.** Some do need help

coming up with suggestions and options. If this is the case, please make your suggestions helpful by including practical and realistic examples.

RECAP

1. **Restate and go over the decisions the client made.** At the end of the coaching session, as well as any next steps and actions. Take note of the action items, not the negative points of the other person's behavior. Recap the main discussion points and add anything you've discussed that the person could do differently regarding their decision making, behavior or that might develop their life and recovery skills, avoid misunderstandings, and check to make sure that your communication is clear.

2. **Communicate the goals for the next feedback coaching session.** Be sure that you devote some portion of your agenda to going over the client's recovery goals for the upcoming accountability period. As we've mentioned a few times, one of the core strengths of effective feedback coaching sessions is the ability to integrate the goals and actions of your individual clients with the overall large-scale recovery efforts, including plans and short-term, mid-range and long-term goals. To do this, you need to make sure that your clients know what those other recovery goals are. You want them to keep these in mind while carrying out their assignments and recovery responsibilities. Touching on them during feedback coaching sessions is a good way to keep clients on track with these all-important points.

3. **End on a positive note.** It's important to always wind-up by expressing confidence in the person's ability to improve their current situation. Example: "You've really thought this through properly today. The way you jumped in and came up with the path forward for this is great! I have no doubt that if you do what you say you'll do, that this will be a lot less stressful this time next week. If you remember from last month, when you followed through on that tough problem with Sarah, you did awesome! Please keep taking the initiate on problems like this as soon as you can, so they don't fester like they used to. If they fester, they cause undue stressors and that's a risk for relapse. You definitely don't want that!"

4. **Reiterate your ongoing support.** Coaching sessions can be an opportunity to reiterate your support for the client and their recovery efforts. This is the perfect way to round off a feedback coaching session.

After the Feedback Coaching Session

TAKE NOTES

1. **Agreement:** Take notes during feedback coaching sessions and encourage your clients to do the same thing. Look at what they've written and make sure you are both 'on the same page'. There's something about putting pen to paper that just solidifies next steps! Plus, some clients are 'wiggly'. They will ignore the spoken word session after session. Additionally, if your deliverables and promises and next steps are in writing, that is a 'lock it down' mechanism. Having this will shorten negative discussions. The points are the agreed points. It's not easy to 'wiggle away from' written documentation. This will help you to have a written documentation of what has transpired.

2. **Writing is better than memory.** Taking notes and documenting also helps to secure the points in your and your client's memory, so that they're more easily recalled at a future date. It's all too easy to forget minor points. Taking notes will help to prevent this. It also helps with recovery accountability. How can you remember what people promised to do for themselves if you don't keep notes?

3. **Writing things down makes them 'stick'.** For many Behavioral Sobriety™ Coaches, an important aspect of their service is a session recap that is delivered to the client regarding the talking points and actions steps including any promises made. That which you track, write down and deliver to the client has a

much better chance of 'sticking'. Written words have much more 'weight' than spoken words. If you want the better outcomes for your clients, you'll consistently provide documentation to them after your coaching sessions.

Lay the Groundwork for Praise

A successful feedback coaching session should begin with a result in mind. It should inform the client exactly what he/she needs to do to become better equipped to achieving the recovery goals and objectives that a client is seeking. This gets the client to "listen up" because it directly affects their personal interest and goals for their recovery efforts.

Discuss Strengths and Weaknesses. When discussing strengths and weaknesses during a feedback coaching session, and setting up 'praise', it's often helpful to look to the 'Book About Me' workbook and the 'Report About Me' section on strengths and weaknesses, as well as the SWOT. Make sure that you draw your conclusions from the available facts and not form any 'baseless presumptions'. For example, look at the available data, verifiable actions and behaviors, metrics, and documented instances of the client's behavior to determine what they might need to work/focus on, instead of basing it on something that you heard through the grapevine. Likewise, be sure that a client is doing well in a certain area before you praise or reward them for it, or else you'll inadvertently reinforce unwanted or negative behavior.

Additional Types of Evaluations

Not only is there the traditional 'sit down with Recovery Coach and receive feedback meeting,' but evaluations can take on many different forms. Different forms of evaluation are particularly useful in gathering information that a Recovery Coach may have overlooked, can be used as additional resources for a formal evaluation, and provide the perspective of an outsider.

CLIENT SELF-APPRAISAL/SELF-EVALUATION

Have the client conduct a Self-Appraisal/Self-Evaluation on his or herself a few days before you're scheduled to provide feedback. You should already have the client's 'Report About Me' but this Self-Appraisal/Self-Evaluation should be focused on "How I Think I Am Doing". They should turn this self-evaluation into you, giving you time to go over it before you meet. Be warned that you should always let the client talk through their Self-Appraisal/Self-Evaluation prior to providing your feedback. Sometimes this insight can wreak havoc on a coaching session or significantly help with a Recovery Coach's feedback. But you can't anticipate which it will be until the client provide their personal view of themselves and their recovery efforts thus far.

Self-Appraisal/Self-Evaluation can really be quite a valuable tool, as it can give you unique insight into how the client is expecting your feedback to go. If they're very far off-base, it can help you to better prepare for that. You can prevent emotionally based arguments, and to come up with a strategy to help the client get their perspective back on track with reality. The Client's Self-Appraisal/Self-Evaluation can be an excellent tool for the Recovery Coach to self-evaluate their own effectiveness as a Recovery Coach. How? Think about it. If you consistently see that the clients under you are of the same opinion as you about their performance, you are doing a good job setting expectations, delivering feedback, and communicating about performance. But if they are consistently off base, you might want to look at how you are 'keeping it real'.

PEER REVIEW, STAFF OPINIONS, AND THE LIKE

Peer reviews, staff opinions, and the like are all ways to get different opinions about an individual's behavior in various situations and settings. Because they are simply a 'snapshot' of how the client acts in different situations with different people, the information provided should be looked at in this light. As an example, people tend to be on their best behavior in church. They don't swear or get angry. Ten minutes after the service is over, they might bounce back to their 'normal' behavior. Their preacher might never see this. As such, situational 'snapshots' of behavior should be taken as an important but fallible source, especially if viewed solely on their evidences alone. However, if these 'snapshots' show a lot of people drawing the same conclusions about an individual, they can be thought to be fairly accurate. It is the Recovery Coach's responsibility to provide feedback to the client on any areas of concern that may surface. Don't forget to speak candidly with the client about these concerns but refrain from "naming names".

If nothing else, having an approved list from whom you can gather behavior 'snapshots' should give you a great start in gathering information about how a client is doing (how they are behaving) outside your coaching sessions. If you can put the pieces of the client's behavioral puzzle together, you'll provide better feedback. More information provides better balance in the feedback process in general. It helps a Recovery Coach have further insight about a client's behavior and habits as they work their recovery efforts.

GROUP COACHING SESSION REVIEWS

When a client participates in a Group Coaching session, a different behavior dynamic can be observed. If you are facilitating group coaching sessions, participants can provide insight about other participants with a view to 'lifting' and helping. A survey whereby peer group are encouraged to comment on what behavior they perceive as helpful to recovery efforts pertaining to an individual is powerful information for the client. Peers often have a perspective that others don't. Of course, peer feedback isn't always perfect, but it can shed light on important areas of improvement, highlight strengths that clients may have 'blind spots' about, and/or can provide views about the client's behavior based that person's interactions. Additionally, these should obviously be carefully combed through for biases, but they can nevertheless offer a unique perspective that should not be totally discounted. Remember however, that if the comments are not backed up by solid facts or evidence, you should not use them in coaching sessions as an absolute. They are for discussion and reference.

SOLICITED AND UNSOLICITED FEEDBACK FROM SUPPORTERS, FRIENDS, AND FAMILY

Feedback from supporters, friends and family members is always valuable. Why? Because patterns emerge. The more 3rd party feedback you can get, the better the data points. An integral part of recovery efforts is how the client's behavior appears from another person's point of view.

A reminder: Be sure to keep within all confidentiality laws and guidelines when gathering and discussing any client information. This is very important from a legal and ethical standpoint. A good rule of thumb when soliciting 3rd party feedback is to take information in but never give information out without express permission from the client to do so. Whenever you have permission to reach out to others for solicited feedback, it is often best to have a standard form or survey – either printed or electronic – which details what the feedback will be used for and who will be provided with an information. This ensures that the person understands what types of information you are looking for and gives them a sense that providing this information is part of the process. In other words, it puts them at ease and builds trust.

While any 3rd party information should be scanned for biases and other indications of less than ideal information (perhaps gossip or incorrect information), they are often very reliable glimpses into a client's behavior and 'temperature'. Unsolicited feedback can be even more interesting as it implies strong feelings on behalf of the person providing it. After all, they went out of their way to contact you with their information, without your even having to ask. Again, you must check and verify against other information and observations and discuss these with the client without breaching confidentiality on either side. Remember to ask what information you are at liberty to disclose and discuss and any considerations or boundaries in that disclosure. This is important because it sets up an environment where information will continue to flow.

COUNSELORS, THERAPISTS, AND COACHES

As a Professional Recovery Coach or Sober Coach, you love helping people and enjoy teaching others how to stay sober and enjoy life. You deserve to be paid for your time and efforts. We offer a reputable program that is cost-effective and recognized in the industry. We offer continuing education that is great for therapists, drug and alcohol treatment staff, admissions counselors, after care staff, business developers and marketers, social workers and addiction professionals. At The Addictions Academy, we offer Mentorship programs, Certifications and Training programs for Therapists, Counselors and for those in Recovery themselves. A Recovery Coach job can be rewarding and lucrative and our Recovery Coaching Course or Sober Coaching course will teach you all the essentials you need to succeed in accepting new clients or adding clients to your existing practice. Our Recovery Coach Certificate Program will prepare you for the real world and clients that are ready to hire you with your new level of expertise as you become a Recovery Coach.

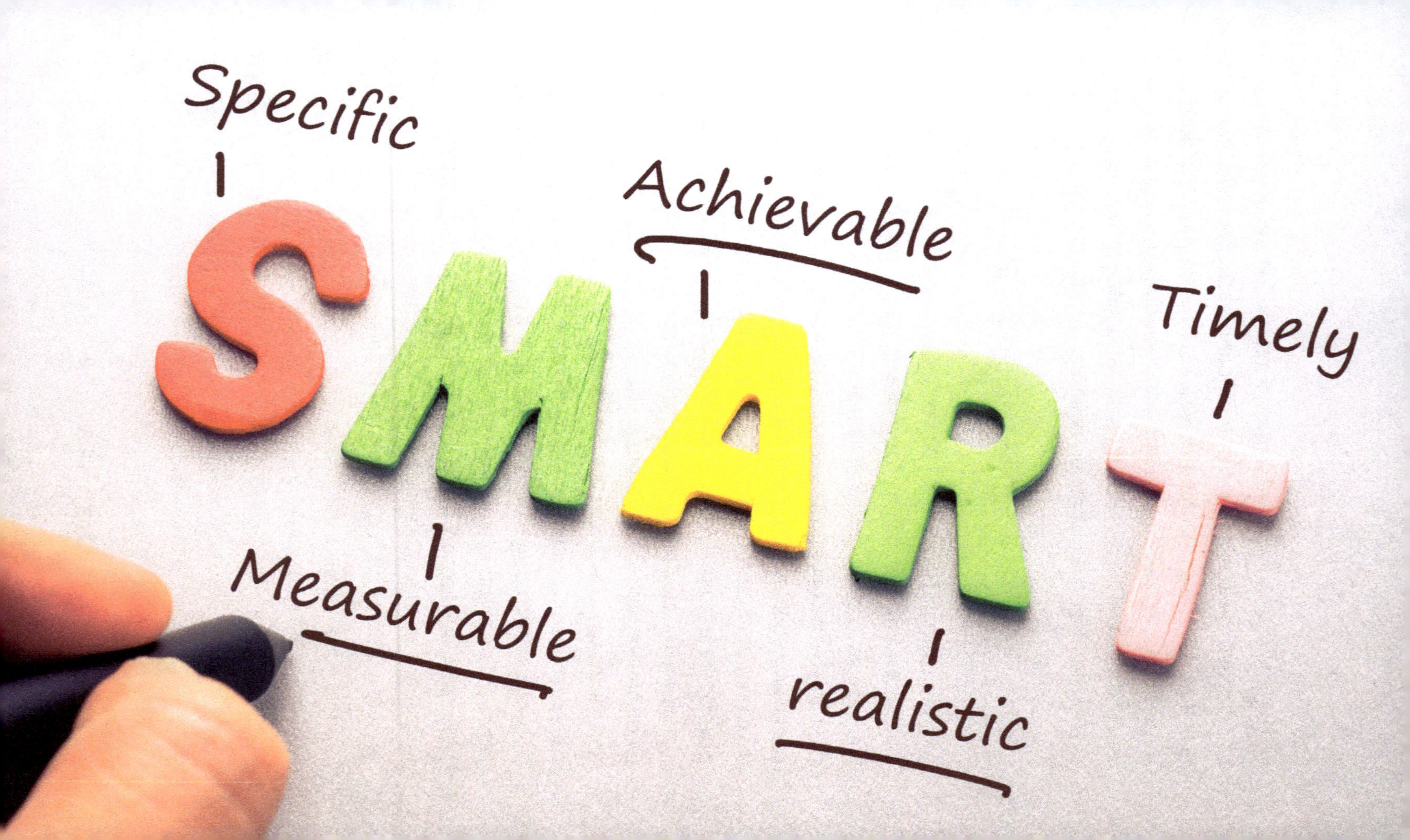
Specific
SMART
Achievable
Timely
Measurable
realistic

Goal Setting and Recovery Accountability

The Definition of a Recovery Goal

Accept responsibility for your actions.

Be accountable for your results.

Take ownerships of your mistakes.

A recovery goal is defined as "an agreed upon statement of what should be achieved within a defined period of time". The goal should be broken down into SMART components detailing what the responsibility is, what the recovery accountability expectations are concerning results, and authority or decision-making guidelines. When these are fleshed out, they'll paint a great picture of what the client's overall recovery efforts should be focused on, so that they have individual goals that all add up to overall strategic goals.

Part by part, let's look at what this definition means:

"**An agreed upon statement**" means that both the client and the Behavioral Sobriety Coach must agree upon the goal for it to be effective. A goal that is imposed upon an unwilling client is the kind of goal that isn't going to generate the necessary excitement for accomplishment. Nevertheless, sometimes you all must accomplish goals or tasks that you don't agree with. The key here is to have both parties agree that the responsibility will be carried out to the best of their abilities.

"**What the client will achieve**" implies that the goal must contain some sort of concrete, achievable objective leading to an outcome. A goal without specifics is unthinkable. You recommend making certain that all goals have metrics attached and that the parties discuss these prior to deployment, and that these be detailed in a SMART format.

"**Within a defined period of time**" indicates that a goal must have a specific deadline. Goals without deadlines tend to fizzle and die out whereas deadlines produce a great deal of enthusiasm and excitement, as well as results. Plus, often clients who want to please you (and others) and who want to 'win' will do things ahead of time. But if they don't know what timeframe they're driving toward, you can't congratulate them on this.

SMART Goals

SMART is a good acronym to remember while setting goals for the next recovery accountability period. Ask whether the goal is…

- **Specific**. The more specific a goal is, the more objective and concrete the measurement of its success will be. It does no good at all to have a goal where you can't even tell if it's been achieved or not. Establishing very specific conditions for success will give the client a strong sense of something to work towards. It will make it much easier to break the goal down into smaller, progressive units and/or sub-goals.

- **Measurable**. A good goal must have some ability to measure whether it has been reached. A good example would be something like "read 15 pages of the workbook and complete all the activities by May 7th", because this offers some clear-cut criteria of completion. 14 pages would mean failure, whereas anything at or above 15 pages would mean success. It's very simple and clear-cut, and easy to measure using simple numbers. This is the best kind of goal to make; one where there can be no arguing or equivocating about whether it was achieved. That should be self-evident. People may argue that some goals are difficult to measure. This is indeed true. But, trust me, if you don't spend some time defining adequate metrics and measures of successful behavior and/or performance, you'll spend much more time later bickering with clients come feedback time. Be warned: This is time well spent!

- **Achievable**. A good goal must be achievable. It must have a result that is possible given the time and resources that the client must work with. Asking someone with a limited time to read and work through 125 pages in a week is senseless. They just can't be expected to deliver. It's unreasonable and sets the client up for stress and/or failure. You'll only frustrate everyone involved. The point is that if a goal cannot reasonably be achieved, it is not a good goal.

- **Realistic**. Much like the previous requirement, realism is a critical aspect of a good goal. There may be certain goals like "make peace with every member of your family in the next two months" that are theoretically achievable, thus satisfying the third condition, but just aren't very realistic. It normally takes a long amount of time for anyone to repair relationships. Eight weeks is a short period of time. Unless there are some serious extenuating circumstances, it's not reasonable to think that this is a realistic goal. All goals should be analyzed to make sure that they're realistic in the context of the recovery efforts and support network/environment that they must be attempted in.

- **Timely**. Lastly, a goal must be timely, which is to say that it must have a somewhat pressing deadline that establishes a sense of the appropriate urgency to get it done. Goals that are set for several years in the future tend to never get accomplished, because it's simply not possible for humans to hold focus on something for so long. set Try to set goals that can be accomplished within the next performance period. If they are longer range in, make sure that you and the client always set benchmarks against the longer-range goals so that you can track progress. For a goal to be a driving force, it must have an appropriate sense of urgency. Good goals must have a somewhat strict time limit. Check to see if your client's goals do. If they don't, consider walking the client through how to break the bigger ones down into smaller segments with a series of deadlines that feed into the larger goal. When you do this, make sure you keep all timelines and metrics focused on the overall anticipated result. Tie them together to achieve success in the next recovery accountability period.

Gain Commitment to Self-Improvement

It does no good for your client to set recovery goals if your client is not committed and/or passionate about meeting them. They need to know that meeting their recovery goals is not just a matter of helping themselves in the short-term. Making a commitment and achieving goals consistently leads to better habits, and a better life overall. The degree of commitment a person has impacts health, relationships, and so much more. As such, it helps to end each coaching session by getting the client's firm commitment to the principle of self-improvement and growth. If you're able to motivate them to improve themselves through their education and recovery efforts, then it'll be much easier for them to meet the recovery goals that they want. If you concentrate on the principle of driving motivation and commitment, you will see results in this area.

Identifying and Removing Roadblocks

A key part of Recovery Coaching is setting the stage for your clients to succeed. In many instances, this is largely dependent upon the efforts of the Recovery Coach to identify any roadblock that could happen in the next performance period. After you set goals for the next performance period, look at those projected goals and help walk through and identify possible upcoming roadblocks. This is a key component to goal setting because the goal should be attainable. A good Recovery Coach will be able to question the client about any potential roadblocks that stand in the way of accomplishing goals. Once uncovered, a plan must be sought to overcome and /or remove them, or at the very least they can discuss ways to deal with them.

A Recovery Coach must facilitate the client to succeed. This means that all obstacles must be first identified, and then a plan discussed to remove these or deal with them accordingly.

In this way, Recovery Coaching discussions empower that client to think through and meet goals head on. For example, if a client is given a specific task to complete but finds that the resources he needs to complete that task are not available to him, and this possibility didn't come in the coaching session, then the fault lies squarely with the Recovery Coach. If you expect goals to be accomplished, then the client must have talked through roadblocks and whether they have the necessary resources is a potential roadblock! A Recovery Coach who is practicing good Behavioral Sobriety™ Coaching techniques checks whether all the resources are in place. By failing to identify the roadblock or discussing limited resources and then asking the client about their plan to remove these, the Recovery Coach has failed in their coaching session.

After Action Reviews

An after-action review is an assessment that is carried out after a major goal has been met. It is basically an attempt to look at how the result or outcome of a goal came about, what factors contributed to it, and how it might have gone differently. The goal is to assess anticipated results versus actual results. Obviously, this can be a very useful tool when it comes time for feedback and/or formal client evaluations. After a goal is completed, have clients fill out after action reviews regarding the effectiveness of the goals and how smooth the process went while working toward that goal. Set clear parameters that all statements must be based on facts, data, or other evidence - never on opinions. These fresh perspectives can be used to get a sense of what can be done better for the next time. Use information gathered from after action reviews to set goals for the recovery accountability period. Since Recovery Coaching is a continuous process, after action reviews should be conducted after every goals period to continuously improve goals in the future.

Coaching Skills for Recovery Accountability

One of the fundamental pillars of Behavioral Sobriety™ Coaching is holding the client accountable. Evaluation of how the client is going against expectations and feedback is a critical tool for helping to ensure that your coaching sessions are on the right track.

> You might not be able to change the past, the situation you currently find yourself in, or what people think of you right now. But you can be accountable for your future. Accountability is the key to changing everything in your life. When you get serious about accountability, people take notice. Doors open, people help, and your life changes.

We'll also cover the importance of documentation, and of committing accountability reviews to writing. One objective of recovery accountability is to help clients grow through feedback and coaching.

Then, we'll discuss the importance of setting goals for the next steps to ensure future success. These aren't just any goals, but reasonable, attainable goals that strengthen the client's motivation, build self-confidence, foster great decision making, and enhance life skills.

The Definition and Goals of Recovery Accountability

RECOVERY ACCOUNTABILITY

To be successful at holding oneself accountable, you must first know exactly what recovery accountability is. To put it simply, recovery accountability is an 'ongoing process' by which you set goals, cultivate skills and appropriate behavior, put these into practice while driving toward a specific measurement. Recovery accountability also encompasses providing information and feedback to clients based on the three fundamental areas:

- Functioning in the situations they find themselves in (based on predetermined expectations)
- Conduct and behavior (how the client acts in the situation)
- Willingness to participate and engage.

The definition of recovery accountability is rather lengthy, but it's not complicated if you take a moment to break it up.

RECOVERY ACCOUNTABILITY IS AN 'ONGOING PROCESS'.

This means that it's something that should occur minute-by-minute, hour-by-hour, day-by-day, not just during the coaching sessions. Recovery accountability should be one of the foremost considerations of the relationship between the Behavioral Sobriety™ Coach and their client. Recovery accountability is not something that is pushed aside to be dispensed with as a chore only when things don't progress as planned. It's an ongoing process that provides continuous timely feedback to the client; both positive and when things aren't on track.

PROVIDING RECOVERY ACCOUNTABILITY FEEDBACK HELPS CLIENTS STAY ON TRACK BECAUSE OF A UNIVERSAL PRINCIPLE: THAT WHICH GETS MEASURED, GETS DONE.

RECOVERY ACCOUNTABILITY INVOLVES MOTIVATING AND CULTIVATING CLIENTS.

To motivate a client, they must have sufficient reasons to meet a specific goal. But often that isn't enough, clients need to know how they're doing before that goal is completed. Ongoing feedback is critical in improving the client's overall life skills and behaviors. When you say that you cultivate a client, what you really mean is that you're availing that client with the tools or resources that he or she needs to be successful. You're helping foster the conditions by which they can become as successful as their potential allows them to be. The feedback that is generated from recovery accountability must be linked to suggestions and strategies for their ongoing recovery efforts. These must be equally motivating and empowering in the client's eyes.

Recovery accountability provides feedback in the three key areas whenever a client sets future goals:

- **Functioning:** Appropriately 'functioning' is a concept at the core of Behavioral Sobriety™. In the situations the client will find themselves in, it is vital that they are able to perform well. Clients must 'function well' when working with others, communicating, and carrying out their day-to-day responsibilities so they can thrive. Operating their life well means they must 'function' as an adult, taking on the behaviors that are required for each circumstance they are addressing. Functioning in society is based on predetermined expectations of things the client must do. It is a 'catch-all' term for their responsibilities to themselves and others. The coach and client must determine and agree upon what is expected of the client, so they can measure their recovery efforts accordingly.

- **Conduct and Behavior:** Conduct and behavior is how the client performs in a situation. It is 'how they function'. Clients are different in their approach to getting things done. Two clients can get similar results by doing things very differently. And that's ok! Conduct and behavior encompass factors like personality, attitude, communication style, and how the client interacts with others. It doesn't make any sense to clients working hard on their goals, if their efforts run contrary to tried and true recovery efforts or that don't work for their support network or family. Part of goal setting and recovery accountability is making sure that everything is in sync.

- **Willingness to participate and engage:** No one can force a client to participate. The degree of participation and willingness often reflects how well a client will do with their recovery efforts. NOTE: As the client gets some 'wins' under their belt, you might see their willingness to participate and engage go up.

RECOVERY ACCOUNTABILITY EVALUATION

When you say that a client evaluation must be **"carefully considered,"** you mean that a good deal of preparation must go into the evaluation. A coach should not take the matter lightly. And remember, the goal with evaluation is to analyze expectations versus actual results.

"**Objective judgment**" means that the conclusions you come to must deal entirely with facts and recorded instances of how the client functioned and behaved based on expectations, and their willingness to participate. Findings and feedback must deal specifically with recovery efforts' related issues and goals. These can never take the form of a personal attack. Likewise, a recovery accountability evaluation should never be expressed in a subjective way, with the coach saying things like "I think..." or "I feel**..." One should be able to point to specific facts about the client's actions and/or behavior not their character**.

"**Consistently applied**" means that client evaluations must be based on a consistent standard. In this way, all feedback will be given equitably. By offering continual and timely coaching feedback, you can keep stress levels lower. Having feedback 'build up' isn't good for the coaching relationship. Stress builds as time goes on. The client might feel that you are 'keeping score' or are holding back only to unleash a torrent of feedback all at once. This can-do damage to the coaching relationship in a variety of ways.

RATING THE CLIENT

The result of your analysis of how the client is doing is a 'rating against expectations'. Most coaches don't really like to give clients a rating, but this coaching responsibility is important. Clients need to understand exactly how well they are doing, and rating how well you think they are doing versus expectation is a big part of that. This process is painful for some coaches. They simply do not like ranking clients. It's understandable, but you must do it. But it's part of your responsibility as a coach. Think of rating as an objective way to provide impartial and critical feedback. If you can't measure and rate expectations versus actual results, it's just about impossible to provide great feedback. A rating system or ranking process is a useful tool because it allows for the clients to set goals more effectively and provides the motivation for self-improvement. Also, if the client is just starting out in their recovery efforts, your rating should allow for 'wins'. Expectations that are too high can be harmful as those that are too low. As a Recovery Coach, you must gauge where the 'bar' is and adjust accordingly in your coaching sessions. **Providing feedback while sustaining motivation is often a delicate balancing act.**

While it is often stressful for clients to go through this process, there are usually multiple benefits and rewards for high achievers and clients who perform well. Also, if clients are not performing well against their expectations, this must be discussed, and a plan put in place to adjust things. For this reason alone, many Recovery

Coaches and clients come to accept the rating process as vital to the process.

TYPES OF CLIENT RATINGS

In Recovery Coaching, it's best to keep the rating process simple, so we suggest you use these four generally acceptable ratings:

1. Far Exceeds
2. Exceeds
3. Meets Expectation
4. Needs Improvement.

People can be at 'meets expectations' in one area, 'exceeds' in another, and still rate a 'needs improvement' in yet another. Most important, even a client who consistently 'needs improvement' should occasionally meet expectations. These four simple ratings help categorize and standardize recovery efforts. From most desirable to least, they are as follows:

Far Exceeds Rating

The Far Exceeds rating is given when the client succeeds and goes above and beyond what they promised to do. They might have even amazed you. If you've agreed to an assignment or task, and it was completed swiftly and decisively, with an unmistakable flair, they get a far exceeds ranking. This is the ideal that all shoot for, but realistically speaking, it is not an attainable goal for just anyone or all the time. Several factors must line up for one to operate at this level, especially consistently. Nevertheless, the far exceeds ranking for assignments and promises is a dream come true for any Recovery

Coach because congratulating and recognizing great recovery efforts is awesome! These make for the easiest feedback coaching sessions as you usually never run into any issues, problems, or conflicts.

When a Recovery Coach provides a far exceeds ranking in a coaching session, the client should be proud. Documenting these consistently allows the coach to establish a record of the client's high performance. It also shows them what path to take to continue advancing their recovery efforts towards higher goals. When a client consistently shows they can achieve at a certain level, you can systematically 'raise the bar'.

Exceeds Rating

A Recovery Coach should be able to spot those clients who are consistently performing that are above expectations. In fact, the best Recovery Coaches, through holding clients accountable over the long haul, can create this type of client! Great Recovery Coaches see their clients' potential and then motivate them to become more successful. Consistently meeting and achieving recovery goals needs motivation and that comes from hope and support. Remember this: The 'exceeds' client demonstrates the capacity of exceeding expectations most of the time but doesn't always manage to do so. So be gracious and kind in your feedback. The client is learning how to overcome a lot of things from their past. They might also exceed expectations occasionally; and surprise you and themselves! Exceeds for them is not yet consistent. However, they usually never fall below meeting any coaching session expectations if their Recovery Coach and support network are strong. Clients typically achieve more than they could have on their own when they feel people are 'in their corner.

Recovery Coaches look for success and are great at identifying and singling out this type of client's efforts. Success breeds success, but only if it's recognized. A word or two of heart-felt praise does wonders to motivate clients. In doing so, you can draw out the client's individual talents. A good Recovery Coach can help motivate clients to achieve the most they can, whereas otherwise they might have floundered for years without finding their footing, constantly moving between exceeding and meeting expectations and never consistent enough for great lifelong habits to 'stick'. If left alone, these high potential clients may become frustrated so it's critical to grow and coach them through positive reinforcement and well-considered feedback. The recovery efforts and success with this type of client can be substantial with some well-placed words of encouragement.

Performance Recovery Coach is useful to the high potential client because it lets him or her know exactly what needs to be done to reach his or her true potential.

Meets Expectations Rating

The most common type of long-term client is the kind who lives up to most expectations, getting assignments done and on time. But with little to distinguish them from the crowd one way or the other it is difficult to recognize and reward them other than with standard praise for keeping steady with their recovery efforts. This, however, is in no way to be thought of as bad. After all, the recovery work is getting done, isn't it? The individual is living up to recovery effort expectations admirably and should be praised for it. A Recovery Coach can certainly help the 'meets expectations' client by challenging them with new goals or assignments that test their limitations. This should be done to keep them feeling actively engaged with their recovery efforts. And remember, when they are successful, tell them you are proud of them! "Meets expectations" clients might never ascend to a higher level, but that's fine, if they understand that it is within their power to work to succeed and thrive in life. Plus, as they get comfortable with their progress they might want to step it up and work at becoming consistently better. Explain what it would take and let them know that you would support them if they chose to do so. Remember, meeting expectations is good. If they continue to get their assignments done, and mend their relationship with self and others, that's the bottom line, isn't it?

THE "MEETS EXPECTATIONS" CLIENT WILL FIND FEEDBACK USEFUL BECAUSE IT LETS HIM OR HER KNOW EXACTLY WHAT IS EXPECTED OF THEM, SO THAT THEY CAN BE CERTAIN THAT THEY'RE FOCUSING ON THE THINGS THAT ARE IMPORTANT FOR THEIR RECOVERY EFFORTS ALWAYS.

A word of caution however. Many "meets expectations clients" can become resentful if they feel entitled to the same treatment, recognition or rewards as high potential clients. This is particularly important if you are running group sessions. Individually, and IN PRIVATE, you must explain what it would take for them to become a high potential client. You must also provide feedback that they are at "meets expectations" and not at "exceeds" so that there are 'no surprises' when it comes time for feedback and evaluation.

Needs Improvement Rating

The "Needs Improvement" rating, on the other hand, can happen often during the early stages of recovery. When people 'slip' while trying to change habits, their effort 'needs improvement'. This also occurs when a client occasionally suffers some difficulties in getting assignments done or promises delivered, on time or at all. One of the biggest benefits of working with a Recovery Coach is their ability to turn around 'needs improvement' clients by holding people accountable on an ongoing basis. Sometimes, it's as simple as weekly coaching sessions and making sure the client knows someone is in their court tracking their recovery efforts. Don't discount or overlook this critical function you play in the client's recovery efforts.

If the client is consistently in the 'needs improvement' zone, a Recovery Coach needs to assess the current goals and recovery accountability parameters. It could be that they are just too high for where the client currently is in their recovery efforts. The goal is to build confidence and set the client up for some 'wins', thus proving that they have the capacity to get on track. It is the responsibility of the Recovery Coach to work with these clients to **identify exactly what problems are holding them back**. Then they must provide feedback and suggestions to help them to overcome those 'needs improvement' ratings. Typically, with the right degree of Recovery Coaching, a "needs improvement" client will eventually become a perfectly acceptable "meets expectations" client, someone who is an asset to their community. A word of caution; not everyone can be motivated towards acceptable performance. You must understand that your efforts must yield a return on investment. Keep this in mind when you decide how much time and effort you allocate to every client. Without this kind of intervention, however, they might have trouble initiating themselves and could eventually get discouraged and sink to the lower level…

The bottom line: The "needs improvement" client can benefit from performance Recovery Coach because it illustrates to them precisely what they need to do to get back on track and become a productive member of their community. Be aware that this is often the most frustrating type of client to manage. The best approach is to be extremely clear about expectations and specific measurements you will use to gauge their performance, behavior, and expectation of improvements. You must be sure to document all conversations, metrics, expectations, timelines for improvement, and goals. Without this you cannot provide appropriate feedback. Unfortunately, you might need this if your feedback doesn't get results or willingness to improve.

WHEN 'UNDERPERFORMING' IS SITUATIONAL, TEMPORARY, OR EVENT-BASED

It's often the case that tough feedback takes place soon after stressful events, new behavior or discussions, or when things are changing in the client's life. The result in this case is that sometimes the cause of the client's 'underperforming' is situational, temporary, or event-based. When a client is 'still learning the ropes' of new behaviors, even if they were doing great last week in other behaviors, you will have to provide feedback on your observations. You can remind them of what happens when changes take place: cognitive dissonance. You can use this topic as an opportunity to help develop the client's resilience and talk through the effects of cognitive dissonance on behavior and habits.

One of the main strengths of Behavioral Sobriety™ Coaching is that it can be a proactive process. It can prepare clients that 'underperforming' is situational, temporary, or event-based forward with their recovery efforts and create new behavior and habits.

Imagine if you had a client who you know has the potential to be promoted into a position of more responsibility at work. But right now, their anger problems keep popping up. You both realize that this is an area where Recovery Coaching must focus on that promotion to happen. This is clearly a good recovery goal. You can't wait for that promotion to happen before you address this in your coaching sessions! You should work with that client now to make sure they have the skills that they'll need later. Much in line with removing obstacles to performance, making sure that clients are working today to overcome the weaknesses that could cripple them tomorrow is a key part of Behavioral Sobriety™ Coaching.

THE IRREDEEMABLE CLIENT

The irredeemable client is just that. It is the client who has trouble living up to expectations, delivering on their assignments, living up to their commitments, and/or is unwilling to make adequate effort. They consistently turn in work late or never. In general, they have problems with all aspects of their recovery efforts. It is not to say that the irredeemable client is a bad person; it might simply be the case that they're not 'ready'. Whatever the case, if you've exhausted all possible means of turning them around through proper recovery accountability, as a Recovery Coach, it's time to cut your losses and remove them from your roster. It might seem a harsh move, it might not be forever, but in the end, everyone involved will be a lot happier.

A Recovery Coach exit plan is useful in this instance, because it lays the groundwork and provides documentation and a standard process for the dismissal, setting a precedent of fairness and protection against any claims. Sometimes, it will be the case that you need to dismiss a chronically underachieving client. However, every termination is an affair that can easily go awry. Make sure you've given fair warning of your intention to terminate with the client and any other affected people in the supporter ranks. Always refer to your advisors and/or legal counsel when faced with this. Litigation is entirely possible. As such, you should use well-documented logs including any evaluations as a tool to demonstrate that the client was assessed fairly and found to be subpar in fulfilling expectations of the coaching sessions.

SETTING BEHAVIOR GOALS AND RECOVERY ACCOUNTABILITY CONSIDERATIONS FOR THE NEXT ACCOUNTABILITY PERIOD

Setting behavior goals and recovery accountability considerations for the next recovery accountability period is an ongoing process. After a coaching session has taken place, the next step is to set goals and recovery accountability considerations for the next accountability period. Recovery goals help the client to advance towards a higher level of commitment in a concrete way. They let a client know exactly what is expected of them and what they must do to meet or even exceed those goals. Behavioral Sobriety™ is the overall goal. When this overall goal is the focus, sub-goals fall into line. As a Recovery Coach, you should monitor the level of the client's motivation and ongoing commitment to their recovery efforts. It is not enough to keep giving goals that offer the same level of challenge to the same clients repeatedly, coaching session after coaching session. This will never motivate people to excel.

Rather, clients who are meeting their goals must be given new challenges, new education, and new opportunities to shine. They need to see they can 'better their last best' so that their rate of motivation and life skills constantly rises. By increasing these, the clients will continuously feel actively engaged with their coaching sessions and recovery efforts. In coaching sessions, it's important for people to learn new things and be challenged.

Likewise, those clients who are underperforming must see through the coaching sessions that they can 'win'. Small 'wins' while gradually increasing the level of effort required, and setting slightly higher and higher standards to meet, is an excellent way to build confidence in clients. This method of inspiration and motivation does wonders to build hope, too. Clients need confidence so that they can improve. Setting the same level of goals at the same standards over a long period of time leads to boredom and a sense of disengagement. Therefore, be careful which goals you set as a part of your performance Recovery Coach strategy. With that said, let's take a moment to discuss the different types of clients.

NO SURPRISES WITH CONTINUOUS FEEDBACK

As we have said, a major goal of continuous evaluations and constant feedback is so that there are "no surprises" when it comes time for the coach to provide the client with an evaluation. Coaching feedback must be given on a constant, timely, and if necessary, daily basis. If this is done properly, then a client will always have a clear picture of where they stand and what they need to do to take corrective action. Delaying feedback is a risk. It risks relapse, it risks relationships, and it risks trust. Providing continuous feedback is important because it ensures that all clients are on track. Not only does it help the client and their supporters know what goals are being met and which are in danger of failing, but it also helps everyone be motivated, knowing that corrections, if needed will be discussed and dealt with in a timely manner.

A client who receives consistent feedback is a client who will know exactly what he needs to do to further their recovery efforts, and ultimately lead a much better life. Please remember, the worst thing that can happen for any of your clients or their closest supporters is to feel blindsided by the feedback or subsequent evaluation you give them. If a client has been under the impression that he was on track, or even exceeding expectations, only to be told at that they need to improve because they're falling below expectations, this is a bad situation. If you do this, expect conflict or an argument just about every time. Therefore, as a Recovery Coach, poor feedback communication equals poor coaching performance. Even worse, these types of surprises destroy trust and the fault lies squarely with you, the Recovery Coach. Avoid this scenario by making sure that you continuously give the client feedback on a regular basis.

To fully understand this principle of "no surprises", let's look at a few analogies:

Think back to when you were in school. When report cards came out, there were those students who seemed confident in what their results would be, as well as those students who were shocked to see that their grades were less than the expected. The difference is that some students knew the grading process and kept track of the continuous feedback they were given in the form of grades on individual assignments. Using this knowledge, they could anticipate what their final grades would be. Likewise, if you provide your clients with continuous feedback on their recovery efforts and behavior, then they'll have the information they need to move forward with confidence.

Another analogy is to consider what you would do if you had a medical problem. Of course, you would go to a person who was able to fix that problem: your doctor. Likewise, when there is a problem with behavior, there's only one way to solve it: address it with the person who is having the problem. A Recovery Coach must take the problem directly to the client and make them aware of it as quickly as possible, hopefully resolving it just the way a doctor would a disease, before it spreads further and ultimately grows beyond control or repair. The bottom line: how can a client 'fix' something they don't know about?

Recovery Coaching is an effective way to ensure synergy between individual and strategic goals. When a Recovery Coach takes on the role of a coach, they can provide direct, constant feedback. If they're trained to be aware of the goals, they can help to set individuals onto the right path for optimum performance.

Imagine a swim team that has been having a problematic season. Meet after meet, they constantly lose matches, but the coach remains silent. When the end of the season arrives, the coach expresses his terrible disappointment with the team and begins to go over what they need to do to improve their performance the next season. The team members look at one another as a realization dawns on them: If the coach had brought this up after the first failed meet, they could have implemented the changes earlier. They might have had a more successful season. Likewise, it is up to the Recovery Coach to give feedback in a timely fashion, at the earliest opportunity possible, so that problems and expectation issues can be corrected before they escalate into bigger problems.

Resources for Evaluation

When you are conducting a client evaluation, it is of critical importance that you draw all your information, evidence, and data entirely from objective sources. Use facts and information that cannot be disputed or argued about. Never use subjective impressions, uninformed opinions, baseless gossip, innuendo, or hearsay. What kind of sources are permissible, you might ask? There are quite a few good sources of objective information about a person's behavior. Knowing where to look for them for that client (assuming you have permission and authority to do so) often spells the difference between a successful and accurate feedback coaching session or a disappointing or risky one.

The bottom line is that you can gauge definitively if the client consistently met, exceeded, or fell short of their agreed upon obligations and behavior according to expectations if you've kept adequate and appropriate notes and shared these with the client. Having adequate documentation is an excellent way to ensure that you have the facts and evidence to support your decisions regarding the client's promises to do certain things and to monitor their behavior. By establishing 'to dos' and behavior parameters up front, you can deliver the feedback that is so crucial to the client's recovery efforts more effectively.

Documentation and follow up removes misunderstandings about who was supposed to achieve what, and whether they ultimately achieved it.

Examining a client's efforts objectively, and the results of those efforts, will help you make the right decision in determining whether an individual should be given credit for a success, or otherwise held accountable and given corrective feedback.

DOCUMENTATION FOR FEEDBACK COACHING SESSIONS

Let's look at an example of how you would use documentation to hold a client accountable for delivering on their responsibilities. Imagine the client just finished a coaching session and promised to attend at least three meetings the following week. Because the client is most tempted by friends after work, it was agreed that the meetings must be in the evening for credit to this promise. Because they have been less than honest in the past about their attendance, you insist that their sponsor confirm the number and times. Compliance on delivering on these recovery effort responsibilities is easy to track and measure on a week-by-week basis. Plus, it's easy to track over an extended period. As the coaching sessions continue over time, you notice that the adherence to the promise seemed to be inconsistent.

As the Recovery Coach, you've provided feedback several times on this issue. Unfortunately, your ongoing verbal feedback has not been entirely effective. Some weeks are great, others not so much! It seemed that it was just a matter of time before the client slipped their responsibility in this area yet again. The habit isn't 'sticking'. You've also described how important it was to attend regularly and to meet with their sponsor, too.

You begin documenting your findings to put formal written feedback together. On analysis of the info you've gathered, you looked at the client's pattern of behavior and discovered that every time you provided feedback, the client adhered to their responsibilities - but only for a few weeks.

Now at this coaching session, you gather evidence, data points, and relevant facts together to provide a formal evaluation. This type of documentation takes the subjectivity out of your feedback coaching sessions.

EVIDENCE VERSUS EXPECTED RESULTS

Recovery accountability deals with **measurable results**. These measurements, however, must be concerned with the individual's adherence to recovery effort's expectations and goals always.

A client's values are just as important as their goals. Many times, a client wants to be rewarded or recognized simply because they met a goal. It's often more important to note **how** a client achieved that goal. If someone checked the box, but the methods they used go against agreed behavior, did 'things they know aren't right', or their conduct is out of line with expectations, then it can't really be counted as an overall success in the end. Coaching sessions should promote great decision making and great habits. The 'how' is just as important as the 'what'.

DESTRUCTIVE CLIENT BEHAVIOR

Sometimes a client will function adequately in life but engage in behavior that is ultimately destructive to themselves or others. This might be the case in the example of a client who achieves a goal but does so in an unscrupulous manner. It might be ethical, legal, operational, procedural, or security behavior or conduct that arises that causes an issue. Documentation of these can be a good way to identify such behavioral tendencies and correct them before they become a problem. In addition, if at any time during a coaching session or assignment that you consider the client a threat to themselves or others, you must follow the Behavioral Sobriety™ Coach guidelines fully. You must also comply with any legal requirements in your jurisdiction. Please review the confidentiality guidelines for Behavioral Sobriety™ Coaches when faced with destructive client behavior.

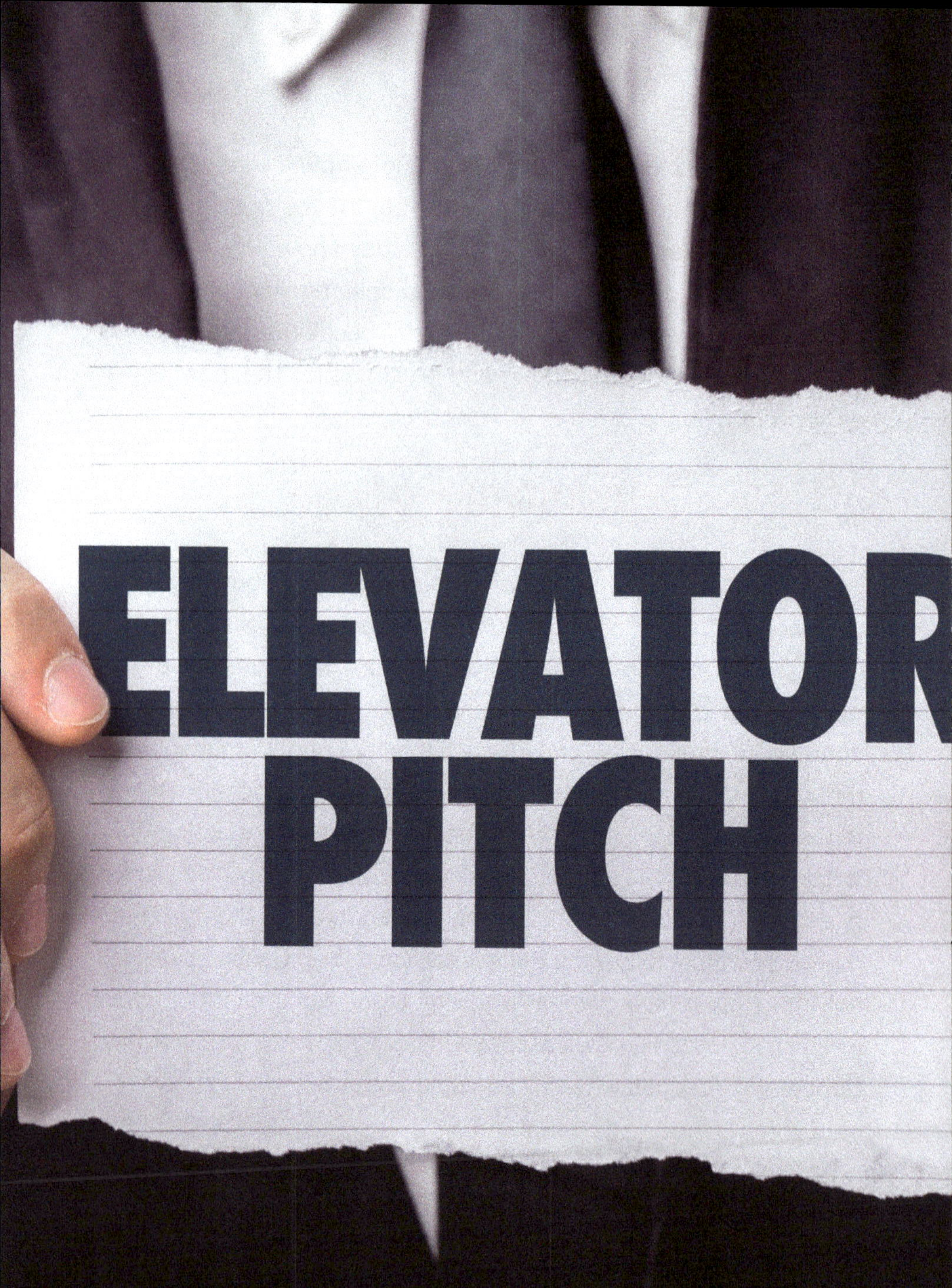
ELEVATOR
PITCH

Elevator Speeches

This section provides a few suggestions for elevator speeches, but always remember that elevator speeches are a way to get a conversation going, so if you're successful, they'll be more of a 'back and forth' with someone rather than a 'monologue' or 'pitch'. To see how this works in a typical conversation, review the example of the 'pitch conversation' following the elevator pitches. IMPORTANT: The reason why you need to rehearse and memorize these points is to ensure they come off your tongue effortlessly when some asks: "What do you do?"

Behavioral Sobriety Coach Elevator Speech

As a Behavioral Sobriety Coach, I work with individuals seeking help with their addiction, helping them overcome any struggles they may face in their lives. This is done on a personal basis and in a group setting, allowing the client to examine their behaviors and thought processes to set healthy, achievable, and maintainable goals. What set us apart in the recovery coaching community is our DISCflex behavioral assessment, which provides an extremely accurate foundation for the client to begin their process of recovery.

Behavioral Sobriety Coaching targets the client's strengths to assist them in achieving long term recovery. This is done through a DISCflex behavioral assessment, giving the client insight to build a foundation of lasting recovery. This is done through the use of accountability, internal self-examination, and guidance through the Behavioral Sobriety Coaching Program.

TURNING AN ELEVATOR 'PITCH' INTO AN OPPORTUNITY TO COACH

If you can fold all your elevator pitch points into a conversation, you'll open a lot of coaching opportunity doors. Here's what a typical "What do you do?" conversations sound like for each of the areas of focus:

BEHAVIORAL SOBRIETY™ COACH "WHAT DO YOU DO?" DISCUSSION

What do you do?

YOU: I'm a Behavioral Sobriety™ Coach.

Are you in the addiction industry?

YOU: I focus on recovery. If you break it down, I help people trying to overcome addiction focus on sobriety.

My nephew has had problems for years. My sister is beside herself dealing with this! He's been in and out of rehab for years and nothing sticks!

YOU: Yes, that's a real problem in recovery. The traditional way of doing things hasn't worked for everyone. Bottom line: There just aren't enough professionals to address this issue. The biggest

problem is that people in recovery need focus and TIME. They need personalized services, and that typically doesn't happen without a dedicated Recovery Coach.

So, what does having someone dedicated to them do? I can tell you, my nephew is a mess and rehab honestly hasn't helped him. It's been a total waste of money! It's kept him from killing himself earlier but honestly, for what we've seen, he's back to square one again! We just don't know what to do, but what we've done before isn't working for him.

YOU: Most rehab programs are a 'one size fits all'. That's what they've had to be because the technology that's been 'the norm' in other fields really hasn't been applied to recovery. Plus, there's just too many people who need help. Nothing's really changed the recovery landscape until very recently. We're now able to get at the core of people's issues with a technology- and behavior-driven program.

What's so different about what you do?

YOU: We actually have a way to get the client's Behavioral DNA in as little as 10-15 minutes. With that Behavioral DNA, we can focus on the unique issues and thinking patterns the person has locked into, and we can address these at the core and start to move the dial on their behavior and habits. That's what I do.

How can you get that much information in minutes? That's hard to believe!

YOU: We have a very sophisticated psychometrically validated assessment and comprehensive reporting engine. It uses extremely complex algorithms but it's simple to use. The goal is for a client to have awareness of their natural behavior patterns. This technology has been used for decades in leadership and management development. So, it's not new, but it's been re-tooled specifically for addiction by the Behavioral Sobriety™ Program.

Why did they do that?

YOU: It's simple. We know that if a person has awareness of things like their behavioral strengths and weaknesses, they can begin to understand what behaviors might help them get and stay sober. The goal is less stress and less chance of relapse.

Do you think that this is that much different?

YOU: Yes, I do. I have seen firsthand what this behavior awareness does to jump start clients in their recovery efforts. When clients go through this it's like a light goes on and they see themselves in a different way. Things become clearer. They get a whole new insight into who they are and why they act the way they do. It's powerful! It gives them insight to stop the 'bad' behavior and lift through their behavioral strengths. I am so blessed that I get to guide them through the process of discovery. With accountability of course!

That must be so inspiring and rewarding!

YOU: Yes, it's one of the most rewarding things I've ever done.